Groceries in the Ghetto

Groceries in the Ghetto

Donald E. Sexton, Jr.
Columbia University

Lexington Books
D.C. Heath and Company
Lexington, Massachusetts
Toronto   London

Library of Congress Cataloging in Publication Data

Sexton, Donald E., Jr.
  Groceries in the ghetto.

  Bibliography: p. 121
    1. Food prices—United States. 2. Grocery trade—United States.
3. Slums—United States.
I. Title.
HD9004.S43   338.1'3   73-999
ISBN 0-669-86199-5

Published simultaneously in Canada.

Printed in the United States of America.

International Standard Book Number: 0-669-86199-5

Library of Congress Catalog Card Number: 73-999

To My Parents

Table of Contents

List of Figures

List of Tables

Preface

While there has been much research on food prices in the inner city, these findings have not appeared in any unified form. I felt there was a need for a *sustained* look at grocery retailing in ghetto areas. To give in one place a reasonably complete and empirically supported description of the inner-city food marketplace is the aim of this book.

The emphasis of the discussion is on what is happening in food retailing in low-income areas. The book does not purport to reveal solutions, but the detailed findings that are presented, I very much hope, may spur the reader to develop policies that will improve the grocery situation in the ghetto.

Most of the material in this book stems from my own research during the past three years. Some of the findings have been published previously in scholarly journals, but much of the material is new.

My thanks go to many: Harold Demsetz who first introduced me to this topic; Harry Roberts and Harry Davis who also served on my dissertation committee (portions of the dissertation appear in Chapters 2 and 3); the Graduate School of Business, Columbia University, who funded much of the work; Linda Haller, Jagdish Sheth, and Ronald Frank who helped me obtain various data; and Jill Hoffman who typed most of the manuscript. Finally, I would like to publically express my gratitude to my wife Mehri, who has on occasion assisted with my research, and who somehow has patience with me.

Donald E. Sexton, Jr.
New York City

1 Introduction

Groceries in the ghetto marketplace have produced considerable and varied reactions:

The charts and graphs that we have prepared . . . point up without question the unfair [food] pricing practices which exist. . . . Mrs. Kenneth Schlossberg, Co-chairman, Ad Hoc Committee for Equal Pricing, Washington, D.C. (99)

There is no truth in the accusation that Safeway charges higher prices or that Safeway raises prices in its poverty stores at the time welfare checks are issued. . . . Robert J. Van Gemert, Assistant General Counsel, Safeway Stores, Inc. (99)

In our Bedford-Stuyvesant community, the residents have been asking themselves on a day-to-day basis, Why is it that they pay such high prices, particularly for food? Mrs. Gladys R. Aponte, Executive Director of the Consumer Action Program of Bedford-Stuyvesant, Inc. (99)

These [retail] prices are the same in the approximately 450 A & P stores in that area [Metropolitan New York], regardless of whether the store is located in a high-, low- or middle-income neighborhood. William Vitulli, Assistant General Superintendent, Eastern Division, Great Atlantic and Pacific Tea Co., Inc. (99)

Sure I have to charge more than a chain store in the suburbs, but my overhead, risks, and losses are a helluva lot more than anybody's in the suburbs. Even with my higher prices, I make less profit than they do. Sabah Najor, Grocer in inner city of Detroit. (62)

At first glance, the above observations may not seem at all consistent. However, this book will establish that, by and large, they are all true and are all very much interrelated.

The Inner-City Food Marketplace

Although more and more of the food sold in the United States is sold in supermarkets, "The dynamic supermarket development . . . crawls at a snail's pace through the narrow streets of the ghetto . . ." (24) Studies have documented the numerous complaints of inner city consumers regarding higher food prices and lower product quality (99,137). For example, one survey reported that sizable proportions

1

of low-income consumers in Atlanta were calling for improvement in their neighborhood supermarkets. Complaints were especially strong among blacks whose attitudes toward their neighborhood super- markets were found to be "25 percent more hostile" than those of whites (137). And when residents of Chicago's predominantly black South Side were asked what additional stores were needed in their neighborhood, 44 percent replied "supermarkets" (140). Such feelings appear even more serious when one considers that fully 20 percent of the income of a poor family is spent for food prepared at home (140).

These complaints can turn to violence. One of the several causes of urban unrest identified by the National Advisory Commission on Civil Disorders was the sharp selling practices by all types of merchants who deal with inner city residents. In food retailing, in particular, there have been several examples of virulent dissatisfac- tion with inner city stores. In St. Louis, the unsanitary conditions at one store had resulted in several warnings from the City Health Department. Early one Saturday morning a Molotov cocktail was thrown into the store and the store was burned out. That this type of animosity is selective and therefore not wholly unreasoning was apparent in the aftermath of the Watts riot of 1965. All the stores of one chain had been burned down, while stores of other chains were untouched (99).

Complaints by black consumers about food marketing usually concern food and store quality and price discrimination, including alleged actions, such as increasing prices on the days that welfare checks are issued or stocking relatively fewer "specials" in inner city stores (99). The primary aim of this book is to empirically examine the grocery market in the inner city and to determine what causes may be underlying these complaints. The motivation for this study is reflected in Congressman Rosenthal's remarks:

It is my personal conviction that equal justice in the marketplace is hardly less important to the poor than equal justice before the law. Price discrimination is intolerable under any circumstances, but particularly so [when it concerns groceries bought by the poor] . (99)

Plan of the Book

Specifically, this book first investigates the extent to which food prices are higher in the inner city; second, examines the causes of any de facto discrimination in price and quality that may exist, and third, suggests ways of determining the forms of food retailing structures for the inner city that are more efficient overall than the current ones. Most of the empirical support for these investigations concern Chicago in the decade of the 60s.

Chapter 2 discusses the research difficulties present in attempting to gauge the condition of the grocery market in the inner city. Previous studies of ghetto food prices are reviewed, and many are found methodologically flawed. Chapters 3 and 4 report price comparisons made among stores throughout the Chicago Metropolitan Area.

Since the food-retailing problems of ghetto areas appear to be due primarily to the retail structure of the inner city, composed of numerous small stores, the next two chapters focus on the basis for such a structure. Chapter 5 looks at grocery retail structure from the viewpoint of the shopper. A model of food-shopping behavior is built from economic theory and is examined with data from a consumer panel. Chapter 6 discusses an economic model of food stores. Data on operating costs and margins for grocery stores are critically surveyed and changes in the number of food stores over time are analyzed to infer profitability.

Chapter 7 describes management science techniques that can be employed to discover alternatives superior to the current structures of grocery retailing found in the inner city.

Chapter 8 summarizes and relates the findings presented throughout.

Price-Setting in Grocery Stores

Some general description of price-setting in grocery stores will provide a worthwhile background for the chapters that follow.

Grocery stores generally appear to vary and advertise their prices on only a relatively few of the thousands of items they sell. If a store were to spread its price cuts over all its products, the decrease might not be perceptible to the consumer. Therefore, price competition among food stores generally takes the form of well-advertised prices on certain products, called "loss leaders," which are frequently purchased and therefore highly visible staple products such as flour, coffee, sugar, bread, milk, soup, and laundry soap. Although most loss leaders remain the same, each grocery store is always looking for new ones (such as nylon stockings) to replace those that have lost their punch because of competitors' actions or reactions. One store manager observed, "you've got to keep getting new people in your store and the only way you can do that is to beat the hell out of the competition on 'ads' and be the first on and the first off promotions" (158). On these loss leaders, the gross margins are usually driven to zero or even to negative amounts.

Holdren (158) and Holton (191) both have developed models of the multiproduct firm that explain this type of competition among grocery stores. Empirically, such behavior has been documented by several studies, including one by Alderson and Shapiro who concluded that when setting their prices, grocery stores weigh the costs of techniques for "creating a [long-term] reputation for satisfactory prices" (79).

The manager of a chain store has much less responsibility for his store's prices than does the manager of an independent store. However, both types of stores are similar in that, typically, prices on only a relatively few items change from week to week.

Chain Store

The chain store manager receives his weekly prices from a central office. He reputedly cannot increase the prices of his store above those centrally determined prices. In many chains, however, the store manager can decrease the price of an item either because he must meet local competitive pressure or because he must move a perishable product. This downward flexibility varies by chains: according to an industry man, who is knowledgeable about the Chicago retail food market, to decrease a price a store manager must petition his area supervisor and the ease with which the supervisor grants permission differs among chains.

Independent Store

The price-making activity of the independent store manager consists generally of continuing the prices of the previous week. In a typical supermarket, there are approximately between 3,000 and 5,000 items: the sheer size of a pricing decision involving all these brands and package sizes, as well as its complexity (most items are interrelated with others), precludes price decisions on each item each week. Just as the chain store prices by exception, the independent store manager usually changes last week's price on only a few items. As Holdren (158) observed, "most of the price-making activity from week to week [in independent stores] involves no genuine decision-making but is the routine application of previous decisions."

The prices of chain and independent stores both can reflect local competitive conditions although the chain store prices may be somewhat more sluggish to respond to changes in competitive activity. According to chain policy, chain store prices should not reflect differences in operating costs among areas; independent store prices can reflect such differences. However, if chains evaluate their managers on the profits earned by their stores, then there is likely pressure on managers in high-cost areas to surreptitiously raise their prices. Therefore, chain store prices do not reflect operating cost differences only to the extent that chains are able to enforce their centrally determined prices.

2

Investigating the Cost of Groceries [a]

In the past six years, several studies have appeared that were directed at the relative cost of food to poor families. A number of these studies—chiefly those performed by the news media and ad hoc consumer groups—have had research flaws so serious that their conclusions must be viewed quite cautiously. Unfortunately, such shortcomings have rarely been noted by the media reporting them. This chapter begins with a discussion of the research design issues involved in comparing food prices; then a number of food price studies are critically described.

Research Questions

There are three basic sorts of questions that price comparison studies have sought to answer. However, researchers have not always understood which question they were answering and that confusion has often led to various methodological shortcomings. The three questions are:

1. Does a particular demographic group *face* higher prices?
2. Does a particular demographic group *pay* higher prices?
3. Is a particular demographic group the *victim* of price discrimination?

The first question concerns the shelf prices for a specific item in various stores. For example, if the price of a one-pound package of brand *X* coffee differs between suburban and inner city stores of chain *A* then one group is facing higher prices. Most price-comparison studies have been based on the shelf prices observed in various stores and, therefore, are directly relevant to the first question.

---

[a] Sections of this chapter reprinted with permission from the *Journal of Marketing*, published by the American Marketing Association.

However, whether families in a given area pay higher prices is a different question than whether they face higher prices. Low-income families, for example, may shop in chain B stores rather than those of chain A or they may not shop in chain stores at all. Similarly, low-income families may not buy one-pound packages of coffee and they may not buy brand X. Any of these possibilities allows the answer to question 2 to differ from that found for question 1.

If one attempts to employ shelf-price data to investigate differences in prices paid, one must weight the observed prices according to some market basket. Such a market basket should be tailored to the demographic groups being studied and should include details on stores visited and products, brands, and package sizes usually purchased. Some studies have used market baskets, but the product weights employed have often lacked empirical support and, moreover, brands purchased and stores frequented have rarely been incorporated in these analyses.

The aim of most price studies, explicitly or implicitly, has been the third question: *price discrimination*. Price discrimination occurs when different prices are paid for the same item by different buyers. For grocery products, items are obviously distinguished by brand, but many price comparison studies have compared price averages composed of different brands. By definition, such studies cannot answer the discrimination question until the various brands are isolated. Grocery products are also differentiated by the services that the store provides, such as check-cashing, credit, ambience, amenities such as water fountains, product assortment, and convenience of location and hours of operation. While such services may differ among stores of the same chain, they are even more likely to differ across chains. Many price investigators have ignored this possibility by collecting and averaging prices from several chains.

Differences in store services (especially among independent stores) make investigating price discrimination difficult. The most obvious way to handle this problem is to measure the level of services offered by stores as well as their prices. Such attempts have been made (96), but generally ratings of services are unsatisfactory since the many aspects of a store are difficult or costly to quantify. A second approach is to consider operating cost data as surrogates for services. For example, payroll as a percentage of sales may be used as an index of employee hours per customer. Operating cost ratios, though, may be unreliable and, in any case, are difficult to obtain on a store-by-store basis. Perhaps the most promising way to examine the discrimination question is through indirect measures such as the failure rates of stores. Areas where food stores are increasing relative to other areas may, other things such as population growth being equal, signify a situation where de facto price discrimination is occurring. Chapter 6 explores such an approach.

Most previous price comparison studies have not explicitly dealt with discrimination. Therefore this chapter focuses primarily on those studies concerned simply with differences in prices charged or paid.

Research Design Considerations

To many well-meaning people, the comparison of grocery prices has appeared a simple matter: assemble some volunteers and tell them to return after they have collected prices from a few stores. Such a casual research design as followed in several studies has resulted in large sampling errors and biases.

The major types of limitations present in various pricing studies concern: (1) sample sizes; (2) selection of store, brand, package size, and day when observation is made; and (3) confusion of shelf prices with prices paid.

Sample Size

Small sample sizes (fewer than nine stores in some studies) obviously mitigates against statistical significance of findings, especially given the amount of price variation normally expected in the same store during a given week.

Store, Product, and Brand Selection

When prices are compared, care must be taken to insure that they correspond to the same thing. Unit prices for a product usually vary by brand and package size and differ not only by independent versus chain, but also by specific chain. Therefore, a comparison is informative only if the compared items consist of the same brand

and package size and come from stores of the same affiliation. Average prices are comparable only if the items in the average are weighted in a similar fashion.

Shelf Prices and Prices Paid

As discussed earlier, if the average price for a product is calculated from a subset of the brands on the market, as an estimate of the cost of food to residents of a particular area, it is biased to the extent they do not buy those brands. In particular, if private brands are not included in the study, the resulting average prices are biased toward equality since the prices of national brands are higher and have less variation over time than those of private label brands (83). In some studies, more than one brand comprised the data for a given product, resulting in averages that are not strictly comparable. Package size may also be an important factor determining price per standard unit and so must be controlled in any study. Finally, when average prices are computed, if various chains, affiliated independents, and un-affiliated independents are not considered separately, biases may result since services vary among stores of different types.

The directions of the biases caused by these omissions vary by study. If private brands, chain stores, or large packages are relatively overrepresented in a sample, the resulting price average is biased low; if underrepresented, it is biased high.

The Price Studies

The price studies described below vary enormously in their statistical credibility. Because of the flaws in the studies undertaken by the news media and ad hoc consumer groups, their results are discussed only briefly in this survey.

Of the media and ad hoc consumer organization studies familiar to the author (56,76,89,91,100,101), all but one concluded that inner city residents are charged more for grocery store products than are the whites or the more affluent who reside in other areas of cities or in the suburbs. However, the methodological errors in those studies were various. For example: Five of these six studies (all but the *St. Louis Post-Dispatch* 91), were based on sample sizes of nine or fewer stores (67). In one three-day study of Safeway stores in Washington, D.C., bias might have been present since just one housewife gathered the prices from three of the stores (100). In a New York study by MEND, selective reporting seemingly was part of the research design since one of the researchers declared, "we wanted to have the most striking differences apparent. We have thrown out surveys in relation to some chains in which we found as many items to be higher priced as lower priced, and this has happened" (10). Controls on reporting errors were rarely apparent—in the Washington, D.C. Safeway study, stores were misclassified into low- and high-income areas and prices for brands not stocked were quoted (100), while in a St. Louis study by the Human Development Corporation over 60 percent of an alleged price difference between low- and high-income area stores was due to a single probable price reporting error (100).

The more methodologically sound studies have been conducted by the federal government, civic groups, and academics. These studies are presented according to the city or cities involved: Buffalo, Chicago, Detroit, Los Angeles, New York, Philadelphia, St. Louis, and various groups of cities.

Buffalo

In the Greater Buffalo area, Teach compared the cost of a 120-item market basket among stores in the urban core, in other areas of the city, and in the suburbs. For each item, the brand and size of each product were designated. The prices were gathered by volunteer students between Thursday and Saturday in each of three weeks. He could not unequivocally conclude either that the poor did or did not pay more since the five different statistical tests he made (for example, analysis of variance) yielded different results (97).

Chicago

Using 1961 *Chicago Tribune* panel data, Frank regressed mean price paid for each of forty-four grocery products against several socio-economic and purchasing behavior variables, including race of purchasing household. He concluded that, "Whites tend to pay higher prices per unit than do nonwhites," but furnished no further details of his results with respect to race (70).

In 1969, the Task Force on Public Aid of the Church Federation of Greater Chicago concluded that a market basket of forty-five items costs most, on the average, in the black inner city areas and successively less as one moved through the white inner city areas to the outer city areas and then to the suburban areas. The results were based on a survey of 108 stores conducted by volunteer shoppers in February and March of 1969. Each shopper was asked to record the price of the cheapest brand of each of the forty-five products. For many products, a particular package size was specified; for others a small range (say, 7-8 oz.) of package sizes. They shopped on whatever day they wished. Included in the inner city store sample were proportionately more small independent stores because that was "where large numbers of public aid recipients could reasonably be expected to shop" (96).

Detroit

Grocery and drug prices and services among stores in the Detroit metropolitan area were compared in 1968 by Focus: Hope, Inc., a civic group sponsored by the Detroit Catholic Archdiocese. The food price survey covered forty-four items, identified by brand and size. Four-hundred inner city and suburban housewives, after six hours of instruction, visited 340 chain and independent stores to gather the price information. In the report, complete results were presented for only nine items. Generally, these items cost the most in inner city small independent stores (the Mom and Pop's), and successively less in inner city larger independents, suburb independents, and suburban chain stores. Aspects of stores such as parking and courtesy were rated by the housewives on a four-level scale (excellent, good, fair, poor) and the independent stores in black and in poor areas were generally found to fall one level below similar stores in white or more affluent areas (68).

Los Angeles

Marcus compared prices of eighty-six food items in thirty-three stores in Watts with those in sixteen stores in Culver City, a more affluent, white suburb. Brand and size were specified for each item.

If the particular brand was not available, the least expensive brand of the product available in the store was included in the survey in place of the brand specified. Marcus found that meat and produce prices were about the same in the two areas, but that for both chain stores and Mom and Pop stores grocery prices were higher in Watts than in Culver City (78). Believing the quality of meat and produce to be lower in Watts than in Culver City, he also concluded that Watts residents in effect paid more for meat and produce.

New York

In the summer of 1967, for each of thirty-seven food items, the price of a leading brand (depending on the brands available in the store) was collected in about twenty-five stores in each of forty-five neighborhoods. Weight was specified for each item—for most, a specific weight, for a few, a limited range (say, 9-10 oz.). This survey was performed by about thirty-five Urban Corps workers (college students), and the data were used in studies by Wright and Alcaly.

Wright compared the cost of a twenty-item food basket across five areas. He concluded that, "If it is true that chains charge higher prices for identical commodities in their stores in poor areas, it did not show up in this survey" (106).

Alcaly concluded that:

the means and standard deviations of the price charged distributions of the individual items were generally found to be not significantly related to neighborhood income and racial composition. . . . In those cases in which significant relationships were discovered—mostly in the smaller independents and among the fresh food items—the mean prices and standard deviations were almost always positively related to neighborhood income. (48)

His principal means of analysis were linear regressions across twenty neighborhoods for all stores, for chain stores and affiliated independents only, and for small independents only. The dependent variables used were the mean, the standard deviation, and a measure of the skewness of the distributions of prices charged for each commodity in each neighborhood. The independent variables were 1960 mean income and percentage of nonwhite residents for each neighborhood. These regressions were made for each of thirty-one commodities and also for a market basket of products.

Philadelphia

In Philadelphia, Dixon and McLaughlin compared the prices of stores in the North Philadelphia inner city with those in higher income areas throughout the city. During one week in 1967, the cost of a twenty-item market basket (composed mainly of staples such as flour and eggs) in supermarkets was found to be higher in the latter areas. Similarly, the cost of the market basket in small stores was observed to be higher in the higher income areas. These patterns were consistent over all of the items in the market basket (64).

Goodman studied the stores frequented by families in a low-income area (about sixty blocks) of Philadelphia as well as the price levels in those stores. For a market basket of seventy-two items, he found that prices in supermarkets were generally higher than those in medium-sized independent stores but were generally lower than those in small independent stores. From a survey of 520 residents of the area, he estimated that 92 percent of families in the low-income area left the neighborhood to do their principal shopping. His conclusion was that, "Because they shop at competitive stores, going outside their residence area to do so if necessary, the poor do *not* pay more for food in this area" (71).

St. Louis

In 1967, Conway examined a pair of stores for each of four chains—one store in the inner city and one in the suburbs. Each store was visited nine times over a six-month period on Thursday, Friday, or Saturday. Prices were gathered for each of fifty items. Conway concluded that, "no unequivocal statement can be made that national food chains charge different prices in poverty area stores as compared to non-poverty area stores" (55). In fact, the cost of a fifty-item market basket in a given chain on a given day was found to be higher in the nonpoverty area store more than twice as frequently as in the poverty area store.

To examine the charges raised in St. Louis in 1967 by consumer groups and newspapers, the Better Business Bureau of Greater St. Louis made an extensive study of retail food selling in that metropolitan area. Over a five-month period, sixty-four chain stores including thirty in poverty areas were shopped a total of 238 times

(169 shopping trips to poverty area stores) by nineteen shoppers. The prices charged for eighteen items specified by brand and package size were collected. For three of four major chains, "no pattern of price differences [was] found between stores of the same chain located in poverty and in non-poverty areas" (50). The prices charged in the seven poverty area independent stores surveyed were generally higher than those in the nearest poverty area chain store on the same day. The Better Business Bureau further concluded that "there appeared to be no consistent pattern of difference between the quality of produce offered in the poverty areas of the suburban areas," and it reached a similar conclusion about meat.

Group of Cities

In 1966, the Bureau of Labor Statistics compared the prices of eighteen food items in food stores sampled from high- and low-income areas of Atlanta, Chicago, Houston, Los Angeles, New York, and Washington, D.C. They:

found no significant differences in prices charged by food stores in low-income areas versus those charged by stores in higher income areas when the same types of stores (chains, large independents, small independents), the same qualities of food, and the same sizes of packages are compared. Prices are usually higher, however, in the small independent stores which are most common in low-income neighborhoods, than in large independents and chain stores which predominate in the higher income areas. (98)

The Department of Agriculture surveyed the prices of two brands for each of seventeen food products in two chains selected in each of six cities. A total of 134 stores were visited in areas classified as high or low income. The study made comparisons only between stores of the same chain in a given city. They discovered "no identifiable patterns of differences between sample stores of the same chain operating in high and low income areas" (101).

The conclusions of the Federal Trade Commission study of stores in Washington, D.C., and San Francisco were based on two surveys. The first survey covered 137 stores and included about 65 items usually advertised by food stores. The second consisted of 166 stores and compared the cost of a market basket of items across the low- and high-income areas. The Federal Trade Commission found that food prices were generally higher in low-income areas. The primary explanation given was that, "Many food stores serving low-income, inner city areas are small, less efficient, and have higher prices" (67). Chain-store prices were often found to be higher in low-income areas than in high-income areas, but the Federal Trade Commission discovered no policy of intentional discrimination against low-income areas. Overall, no significant quality differences in products were discovered between the low- and high-income areas.

Discussion of Findings

Of the fourteen studies based on relatively sound methodology, only five found that consumers in black or in low-income areas either paid or were charged more for food products. The nine remaining studies found that the black or the poor did not pay or were not charged higher prices.

Although the majority of these studies suggest that blacks are not charged more than whites in stores of the same type (mainly chains), these results seem to have had little unified impact on the public debate of the question, "Do blacks pay more?" Community groups and politicians continue to claim that the black (and the poor) pay more for food. This lack of impact can be traced to the discrepancies between what a researcher means when he says blacks are not charged more and what an inner city resident means when he says he pays more for food.

One deficiency of all but one of these studies is the focus on shelf prices. As described above, shelf prices do not provide a direct answer to the question of whether the poor pay more. In particular, stores of the same type may charge the same prices in all areas, but inner city consumers may pay more if prices in independent stores tend to be higher than those in chain supermarkets and if inner city consumers purchase relatively more at independent stores than do consumers in other areas. As Dixon and McLaughlin point out, "the *prices charged* by chain supermarkets are not a measure of the *prices paid* by the urban poor who do not shop in supermarkets" (65).

Generally, prices in independent stores have been found to be higher than those in chain supermarkets. Each of several studies known to the author found that prices in independent stores were higher than those in chain supermarkets (49, 50, 51, 64, 67, 68, 75,

78, 80, 98, 106, 158). Moreover, independent stores seem to be relatively more prevalent and chain stores relatively less accessible in the inner city (166).

In short, for the same brand in stores of the same type, researchers can find equal prices charged in black and in white areas or equal prices paid by black and whites, but blacks may still have to pay more than whites because the (lower-priced) chain stores are not as accessible to them. The inner city housewife has the choice of shopping at the independents with their higher prices or of paying for transportation to shop at a chain store.

The other reason for the lack of impact of these studies appears to be that while answering the question, "Do blacks pay more?" generally they ignore the deeper and more important, "Are blacks the victims of price discrimination?" That question is examined later in this book.

Summary

Several price comparison studies have been discussed and the consensus of their findings appears to be that inner city residents do not pay more or are not charged more. However, many of these findings are equivocal because of methodological reservations. Moreover, they are narrowly focused—typically not considering the reasons for price differences nor where families shop and why. The remaining chapters present research that provide some answers to those questions.

3

Food Prices in Chicago: 1960 and 1963-66 [a]

This chapter describes a study of twenty-seven products in Chicago and its suburbs. All the price comparisons were made for specific brands in stores of specific affiliations, thereby avoiding many of the methodological problems discussed in Chapter 2. In addition, data for twenty-four of the products covered one year and the data for the remaining products spanned a two-and-one-half year interval. These time periods are much longer than those of the investigations surveyed in Chapter 2, most of which were based on from one to four weeks of data. Following a discussion of the data collection and the means of analysis, the findings are examined in detail.

The Data

The raw data for this study consists of product purchases reported by the approximately 700 families in the consumer panel run by the *Chicago Tribune*'s Family Survey Bureau. All their purchases of twenty-four products during 1960 and all their purchases of coffee, instant coffee, and tea during the interval of Fall 1963 to Spring 1966 formed the data base. Overall, 130,000 purchase records were analyzed.

The *Tribune* panel is a widely known and respected source of data that has been in existence since 1947 (although the families composing the panel have gradually changed over time). The relation of the *Tribune* to the panel is carefully concealed from each family recruited.

Selection of the families who are invited to join the panel follows a quota system. The primary controls are size of family, income, and race; the secondary controls are age of housewife, area of residence, and employment status of housewife. For each primary control,

[a]Sections of this chapter reprinted with permission of the *Journal of Economics and Business*.

three classifications are defined, creating twenty-seven household types. For the reports the *Tribune* supplies its advertisers (for example, brand share reports), a sample consisting of 576 panel households is used. The proportions of the twenty-seven household types among this sample are constantly matched against the proportions for the same types in a current breakdown of the Chicago Metropolitan Area (based on the most recent data available from either a *Tribune* sample or a United States census). Families are recruited to maintain this correspondence on the primary controls. Once the primary controls are in line, the proportions of the households classified according to the secondary controls typically also correspond to the Chicago Metropolitan Area breakdown. As new United States or *Tribune* census data become available, the quotas used for recruiting are updated. For example, the definitions of the low-, middle-, and high-income classifications are raised every few years so that roughly a third of the 576 households fall in each one.

To ensure the availability of the 576 households, about 725 households are reporting their purchases each week. In this 725 household group, the full panel, certain household types such as black families comprise a larger proportion than they do in the Chicago Metropolitan Area (because they have been found to return the diaries somewhat less regularly). The data for this study consist of the purchases of the full panel.

Families receive points for filling in the diaries and these points can be exchanged for merchandise. Bonus points are given, for example, if all the diaries within any two-month period are returned or if members of the family besides the housewife initial the diary before it is mailed. For the average panel family, the annual payment for their cooperation amounts to about $50.

Roughly half of those families invited to join the panel do. [Sudman has noted that his experience with panels suggests that the percentage of invited families that join a panel is independent of the compensation within a wide range (222).] In any year, about 10 percent of the families leave the panel—voluntarily, none is removed by the Family Survey Bureau.

When a family joins the *Tribune* panel, an interviewer personally instructs them how to fill out the diary. For the first three weeks of membership in the panel, the family is on probation. The diaries from a new family are scrutinized; and if any anomalies appear, the family is contacted.

The format of the diary used by the *Tribune* is that of a journal. Particular products are not listed in the diary, but rather the housewife lists all her purchases under broad categories such as "packaged foods, groceries and meats, beverages, all bakery goods," or "fresh fruits and vegetables, fresh and smoked meats, fish and poultry." The diary is filled out weekly and is mailed before Monday noon.

Each reported purchase is recorded on a single Hollerith card. Each record includes the following information:

1. selected demographics of household (race, family size, family income class);
2. household serial number;
3. product purchased;
4. brand purchased;
5. day, week, month, and year of purchase;
6. number of units purchased;
7. container size of units purchased;
8. total price paid;
9. total size purchased;
10. whether or not purchase made under deal; and
11. store category (chain affiliation or independent) where purchases made.

Besides the purchase data, an extensive demographic description is available for each panel family.

Disadvantages

The major problems in the use of panel data relate, generally, to the incidence of recording errors, either when purchases are entered in the diaries or copied from the diaries and punched on cards, and, particularly for this study, to the capability of generalizing results based on panel families to the population at large..

Recording errors due to forgetting may be present in these data, but are not likely to be numerous. Forgetfulness errors occur when products are infrequently purchased or when they are bought by various family members (for instance, gasoline). All the products studied here are frequently purchased food products usually bought during major shopping trips. Moreover, the schedule and the reward system of the panel (bonus points) are set up to minimize the possibility of forgetfulness errors. Transcription errors in prices (made when the diary data are punched on cards) can be empirically estimated and would appear to occur in about .2 percent of the records, a reassuringly low figure.

Families who agree to participate in the *Tribune* panel may differ from the population as a whole. In particular, panel families, who continuously record prices, may be more knowledgeable about prices—that is, may remember prices more accurately—than nonpanel families. If so, for commodities of quality acceptable to them, panel families may make more price comparisons than nonpanel families. As a group, then, panel families may receive more quality for their money or pay lower prices on the average for commodities than do nonpanel families. The prime focus of this study are the mean prices paid by panel families classified by race, income, and area of residence. Only if the difference in price sensitivity between panel and nonpanel families is a function of race, income, or area of residence may that difference be a source of bias in this work.

The purpose of the *Tribune* panel is to provide marketing research information concerning the entire Greater Chicago area, not to investigate the behavior of hard-core ghetto residents. This intent is shown in Table 3-1 which compares summary demographic statistics for the Metropolitan Chicago Area from the 1960 United States Census and from the November/December 1960 demographic descriptions of the panel families.

The higher proportion of black families in the panel is due to the oversampling discussed earlier. Generally the panel families tend to be larger than those in the Chicago population as a whole, and this difference may account for part of the difference in annual incomes between the panel families and Chicago households. (The median *family* income for the Chicago area population, according to the United States Census, was $7,300 in 1960, which is equal to the mean annual income of panel families.) When their occupations are classified as "salaried" or "hourly paid," households in the panel and in the Chicago area on the average are quite similar.

However, the most prominent difference in the table is the higher mean family income for black families in the panel compared to the median income for nonwhite households in the Chicago population. That is, the panel families may include relatively fewer hard-core ghetto residents.

Table 3-1

Comparison of Population and Panel Demographic Statistics

	1960 United States Census			1960 Panel Demographics		
	White	Nonwhite[a]	Total	White	Black	Total
Percentage	85.2	14.8	100.0	82.1	17.9	100.0
Number of persons per household (mean)	3.1	3.6	3.2	3.5	3.9	3.6
Household annual income (median for census, mean for panel)	$6600	$3800	$6200	$7500	$6000	$7300
Occupation index[b] (mean)	1.6	1.7	1.6	1.6	1.8	1.6
Age of household head (mean)	. . .[c]	. . .[c]	. . .[c]	45.8	47.5	46.0

Source: U.S., Department of Commerce, *United States Censuses of Population and Housing: 1960, Chicago, Illinois* (Washington, D.C.: Government Printing Office, 1962), pp. 19, 128, 344, and 453. All census data pertain to the Standard Metropolitan Area.

[a]In 1960, about 97 percent of the nonwhite families were Negro.

[b]If the occupation of household head is classified as "salaried," the index equals one; if "hourly paid," the index equals two.

[c]Not available.

To the extent that panel families may shop at particular stores that differ from those at which very poor ghetto residents shop, the results of this study may be biased when used to estimate the differences between prices paid by blacks and whites. For example, if the independent stores the panel families frequent are generally larger than those the hard-core ghetto residents frequent, the prices paid by the panel families on the average may be lower than those paid by the hard-core ghetto residents.

The possible effects of demographic differences on shopping behavior and therefore on prices paid are considered in depth in Chapter 5. In this chapter, the findings are reported by specific brand and by specific chain, and so differences between high- and low-income blacks are important only insofar as they might affect the price paid for a particular brand in a particular store (for instance, through postponing purchases until a sale occurs).

In sum, the black families in the panel do represent a substantial and important segment of the black population of the Chicago area. Moreover, they live throughout the inner city areas and likely shop at the same stores—although possibly with different frequencies—as do families of the lowest income class.

Advantages

The overwhelming advantage of panel data is the wealth of information they contain. For each purchase, the brand and the affiliation of the store where the purchase was made are known as well as the socioeconomic characteristics of the purchasing family. Such detailed information allows comparisons of prices paid for a particular brand in a store of particular affiliation. Such precision was not achieved in most previous price-comparison studies described in Chapter 2, where prices often were compared without regard to brand or store affiliation.

Analysis

The mean prices paid by whites in the suburbs, whites in the city, and blacks in the city were compared. These three areas are referred to as "Suburb", "Outer City", and "Inner City" (Figure 3-1 and Table 3-2). The Suburb area is composed of all the various suburbs bordering Chicago to the north, west, and south. The Outer City consists of those community areas (among the seventy-five community areas comprising Chicago) with no black panel families—chiefly sections in the north side of the city. The Inner City area consists of community areas with no white panel families—communities on the west and south sides that were in the midst of those sections of Chicago where 25 percent or more of the residents were nonwhite. Although certain findings for other areas of the city (Mixed City) are discussed later in the book, this chapter reports only the comparisons made among the above three areas since they were the areas most pertinent to the price comparison questions.

The mean prices were calculated on a per measure basis (per ounce or pound) for a given brand purchased in a given store chain. For each product, two or three leading brands were examined. The same five store affiliations were considered for all the products: A & P, National, Jewel, Certified (an affiliated *independent* group, that is, independents purchasing together), and all unaffiliated independents.

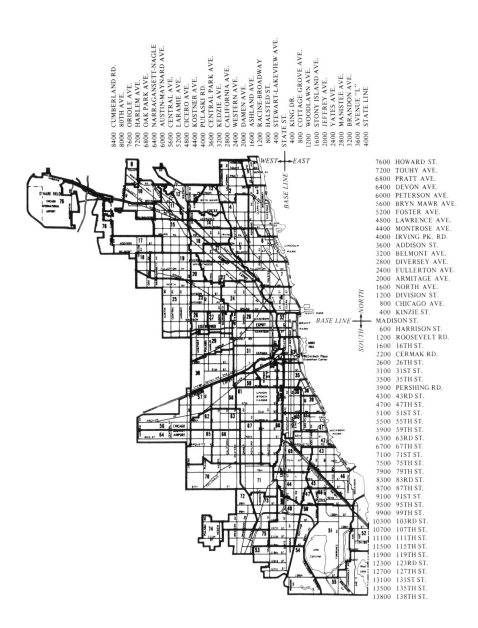

Figure 3-1 Map of Chicago

Table 3-2
Chicago Community Areas

Community	Number	Percentage Nonwhite (1960)	Median Family Income ($000 omitted) 1960
Outer City			
Rogers Park	1	.7	7.5
West Ridge	2	.3	8.9
Uptown	3	4.0	6.8
Lincoln Square	4	.7	7.7
North Center	5	.6	6.9
Lake View	6	3.1	6.9
Lincoln Park	7	4.7	6.2
Edison Park	9	.0	9.2
Norwood Park	10	.1	8.7
Jefferson Park	11	.1	8.1
Forest Glen	12	.1	11.1
North Park	13	3.3	8.9
Albany Park	14	.4	6.9
Portage Park	15	.1	7.6
Irving Park	16	.3	7.3
Dunning	17	.2	8.0
Montclare	18	.1	7.8
Belmont Cragin	19	.1	7.5
Hermosa	20	.1	7.4
Avondale	21	.3	6.9
Logan Square	22	.8	6.7
Hamboldt Park	23	.9	6.8
West Town	24	2.3	6.0
Austin	25	.1	7.6
South Lawndale	30	6.1	6.4
Lower West Side	31	1.4	5.9
Avalon Park	45	.3	8.7
South Chicago	46	5.2	6.9
Burnside	47	.3	6.6
Calumet Heights	48	.2	8.6
Pullman	50	.1	7.0
South Deering	51	.2	7.8
East Side	52	.1	7.4
West Pullman	53	.2	7.5
Hegewisch	55	.4	7.0
Garfield Ridge	56	6.8	7.9
Archer Heights	57	.0	7.6
Brighton Park	58	.2	6.7
McKinley Park	59	.1	6.8
Bridgeport	60	.3	6.2
New City	61	.3	6.5
West Elsdon	62	.0	8.4
Gage Park	63	.1	7.6
Cleaving	64	.1	7.6
West Lawn	65	.0	7.9
Chicago Lawn	66	˙.1	7.7
Ashburn	70	.1	7.4
Auburn Gresham	71	.3	7.0
Beverly	72	.1	11.4
Mount Greenwood	74	.1	8.3

Table 3-2 (Continued)

	Number	Percentage Nonwhite (1960)	Median Family Income ($000 omitted) 1960
Mixed City			
Near North Side	8	33.0	7.0
West Garfield Park	26	16.4	6.1
East Garfield Park	27	62.0	4.7
Near West Side	28	54.4	4.0
The Loop	32	11.5	n.a.
Armour Square	34	52.3	5.1
Hyde Park	41	40.3	6.7
South Shore	43	10.4	7.9
Chatham	44	74.0	7.2
Roseland	49	22.8	7.4
West Englewood	67	11.9	6.5
Englewood	68	69.2	5.6
Washington Heights	73	12.7	8.5
Morgan Park	75	35.2	8.0
Inner City			
North Lawndale	29	91.4	5.0
Near Sough Side	33	77.3	3.3
Douglas	35	92.6	3.8
Oakland	36	98.7	3.4
Fuller Park	37	96.1	4.5
Grand Boulevard	38	99.5	4.3
Kenwood	39	84.9	4.9
Washington Park	40	99.2	4.9
Woodlawn	42	89.6	4.8
Riverdale	54	90.2	3.3
Greater Grand Crossing	69	86.2	6.2

Source: Evelyn M. Kitagawa and Karl E. Taeuber, eds. *Local Community Fact Book, Chicago Metropolitan Area, 1960.* Chicago: University of Chicago, 1963.

Before the entire sample of the twenty-seven products was investigated, a rather thorough examination of three of the products was made (93). In particular, the data were scrutinized for interaction effects among race, income, and area of residence. No systematic or substantial interaction effects were discovered. Moreover, to investigate the effect of time of year on mean prices paid, price comparisons were made for small time intervals—six-month, four-week, and one-week periods. No systematic departures from the findings based on the entire time period spanned by the data were found. Finally, corrections were made to account for differences in average package size purchased, but, again, the findings were not materially altered by the changes.

The relative price differences rather than the actual prices are displayed in Table 3-3, since the relative price differences are much

Table 3-3
Relative Price Differences by Brand

Product Group and Product	Brand	Suburb Price – Outer City Price — Suburb Price					Outer City Price – Inner City Price — Outer City Price				
		A & P	National	Jewel	Cert.	Unaff. Indep.	A & P	National	Jewel	Cert.	Unaff. Indep.
Beverages											
Coffee	A	.06	-.02	-.03[c]	-.04[c]	-.08	-.07		-.05	-.13[c]	.02
	B	.10		.01	-.08[c]	-.10	.04		.07[c]	-.10[c]	.01
	C			-.02					.03		
Instant coffee	A	.13	.06	.03	.21	.08	-.12[b]	-.21	.08	-.13	-.05
	B	.14[c]	.07	-.01	.09	.13	-.30[b]				
	C		.04					-.27			
Tea	A	.01	-.07[c]	.01	-.18[a]	-.08	-.15	.06	.06	-.12	-.14[c]
	B	-.03	-.09	.0	-.07						
	C	.10					-.19[c]				
Soft drinks	A	-.02	-.04	.04	.01	-.02	.04		-.03		-.26[a]
	B		-.01		-.05	-.33[b]				-.21	.0
	C	-.03	.11		.22[b]	-.16[b]				.02	.14
Packaged Goods											
Cereal	A	-.14	-.02	-.27[c]	.09	-.06	.28	.16		.18	-.18
	B	.02	.02	.0	-.01	-.27[a]	.0			.02	
	C	.08	-.05	-.09	-.06	-.31[b]				.01	.19
Coffee creamer	A	.02	.07	.03	-.09		-.13	-.04			
	B			.0							
	C	.03					-.02				

Crackers (Saltines)	A	-.02	.02	.06^b	-.04	-.06	.05	.01		-.05	-.04
	B	-.03	-.10	-.06	-.27	-.10	.15	.16		.05	.05
	C	.16^c	-.15	-.04	.03	-.12	-.19				
Crackers (Graham)	A	.0	.02	-.02	-.03	.05	.03		-.21	.05	.05
	B		.02	.02							-.06
Peanut butter	A	-.07	.05	.05	-.02	-.09^a	.14		.02	-.19^b	.05
	B	.03	-.03	-.03	-.01	-.13^a	.24				
	C	.05	-.05	-.03	-.01	-.08					
Rice	A	.02	.09	.02	.07^c	-.01	.01	-.01	-.02	-.12^a	-.06
	B	-.03					.01				
Salad and cooking oil	A	.03	-.03	-.03	-.07	.04	-.08	-.02	.16	-.03	-.21
	B	-.02	.04	.04	-.15^c	-.15^b	.05		-.26	-.10	-.06
	C	-.02		-.02	-.16^b	-.06				.08	-.06
Salad dressing	A	-.01	-.09	-.03	-.23^c	.04	-.02	.15	-.04	.03	-.23^c
	B		.02	.01	-.09	-.10		-.37		-.14	
	C		.12	-.19	-.31	-.11					
Syrup	A	-.02	-.06	-.06^b	.01	-.09^a	.03		.0	-.05	-.02
	B	-.01	.03	.0	-.03	-.04	.01		.03	.0	-.30
	C	.06	.07	-.06	.0	.04	-.19			-.23	
Desserts											
Dessert pies	A	.0	.07	-.01	.05	.19	.09		.04		
	B		.01	.0	.0	.09	.10				
	C	-.12	-.02		-.58	.25					
Dessert topping	A	-.03	.09	.14^b	.06	-.13	-.02	.02	.17		-.31^b
	B	-.02	.04	.03	-.14	-.03					-.01
	C	.01	-.01	.0	-.06	-.03					
Gelatine desserts	A	.09	-.04	-.45	-.15	.10	-.04	-.33	.09	-.09	-.25
	B	.08	.02	-.02	.02	.03		-.11			
	C		-.02	.03	.11	-.17					

Table 3-3 (Continued)

Product Group and Product	Brand	A & P	National	Jewel	Cert.	Unaff. Indep.	A & P	National	Jewel	Cert.	Unaff. Indep.
Laundry and cleaning products											
Laundry detergents	A	-.03[c]	-.04	.0	-.05	-.06[c]	-.04[c]	.0	-.09[a]	-.14[a]	-.15[c]
	B	-.03			.01	-.07[b]	-.09[b]			-.08[b]	.0
Liquid detergents	A	-.03	.02	.01	.06	-.05	-.04		-.01	-.01	-.03
	B	.03	.01	.02	-.03	-.04	-.04				-.05
	C	.02	-.02	.01	-.03	-.07[c]	.01	.08	.01		
Miscellaneous dry laundry aids	A	.0	-.04	-.02	-.02	-.03	-.18[c]	.0	-.04		
	B	.0	.0	-.06	-.28	-.19[c]		.0	.05		.17
	C	.04	-.16	-.05					.05		
Miscellaneous dry cleaning aids	A	-.03[b]	-.03	-.01	.07	.02	.02			-.04	
	B	-.03[b]	-.01	-.03	-.03	-.05	.03			.06	
	C	.0	-.04	.0	-.09	-.10[c]		-.80[a]			-.08
Other	A	.23	-.02	-.07	.13	-.23	-.08	.18		-.37	-.11
	B	.12	-.02	-.04	-.13	-.17	-.25[b]	-.01		-.01	.0
	C	.08	.10	.04	-.07	-.42	-.14				.0
	D	.15	.05	.06	.06	-.02			-.08		
	E		-.11		.05						
	F	.0	-.09	-.01	-.11	-.07	.0				
Paper products											
Cleansing tissue	A	.05[b]	.02	-.09	.0	-.04		-.03	.05	-.18[c]	.03
	B	-.06	-.09	.05[c]	.05	-.15[a]				-.16	.14
	C			.05							
Food wrappers	A	.06	.05	.01	-.01	-.27[c]	-.02	-.03	.14	.04	.24
	B	.0	.03	-.40	.13	.02		.12			
	C	.03	.06	.04[c]	.12[c]	.03					

Table (product-size intercorrelation matrix; correlation coefficients, lower-triangular form):

Napkins	A	-.02											
	B	.0	-.05										
	C	-.09	-.15	.13									
Toilet tissue	A	.05	.03	.01	-.04ᶜ								
	B	.03	-.04	.03	-.06	.04							
	C	.11	.07	.08	.04	-.04	-.08ᵇ						
Towels	A	-.03	-.02ᶜ	-.01	-.01	-.04	-.04ᶜ	.0					
	B	.05	.01	.05ᶜ	-.02	-.07	-.06	-.20ᵃ					
	C		-.04	-.04	.01	-.04	.04	-.03	-.04				
Waxed paper	A	.02	-.02	.02	.0	-.07ᵇ	-.04	-.02	.01	.03	.0		
	B	.10ᵇ	-.02	.04	.09	-.46ᵇ	-.06	-.04	-.03	-.04	-.37ᵇ	-.05	
	C	-.10	.05	-.08		-.11	.07	-.05	.07		.0		.07

ᵃSignificant at .01 level (2-tail test).

ᵇSignificant at .05 level (2-tail test).

ᶜSignificant at .10 level (2-tail test).

Blank indicates there were no observations for one or both areas.

more easily compared over products, brands, and store affiliations. By finding the median relative price difference for each product and for each product group (Table 3-4), the patterns in Table 3-3 can be more clearly seen.

Findings

Generally, price differences between areas were greater for independent stores than for chain stores. For all but one of the product groups, the chain median difference was smaller than the independent median difference. The relative consistency of chain prices across areas agrees with the statements of chain store executives that store managers in a metropolitan area must charge the same book price unless there is competitive pressure or the threat of product spoilage, when they can charge less than the book price.

Whites in the Outer City purchasing in independent stores consistently paid about 5 percent more than whites in the Suburbs for beverages, packaged goods, and laundry and cleaning products. There was just one major exception to this finding, instant coffee, for which the city residents paid substantially less. Whites in both areas who bought from independent stores paid about the same on the average for desserts and paper products (excepting napkins). Whites in the Suburb and Outer City who purchased in chain stores on the average paid about the same amount for all the products examined.

In city independent stores, blacks on the average paid 10 percent more for beverages than whites (and 15 percent more than suburban whites shopping in independent stores). For desserts, the median relative price difference was also large—17 percent more. For packaged goods, laundry and cleaning products, and paper products purchased in independent stores, Inner City blacks on the average paid 3 to 5 percent more than Outer City whites. Moreover, all these price disparities were quite consistent among the products within these groups. The only sizable exceptions were miscellaneous dry laundry aids and food wrappers.

Blacks buying in Inner City chain stores on the average paid more than whites for beverages (4 percent) and paper products (2.5 percent), but the results for the products in both groups were mixed. For the other product groups, blacks paid anywhere from the same to slightly less than did the whites in the Outer City; but, again, the medians for the products within each group varied considerably.

Table 3-4
Median Relative Price Differences by Product

Product Group and Product	Suburb Price − Outer City Price / Suburb Price		Outer City Price − Inner City Price / Outer City Price	
	Chains	Independents	Chains	Independents
Beverages	.0	−.05	−.04	−.10
Coffee	−.005	−.08	.03	−.04
Instant coffee	.06	.11	−.21	−.09
Tea	−.01	−.08	−.045	−.13
Soft drinks	−.015	−.035	.005	−.095
Packaged Goods	−.01	−.06	.01	−.05
Cereal	−.02	−.06	.16	.02
Coffee creamer	.03	−.09	−.04	
Crackers (Saltines)	−.03	−.08	.03	.0
Crackers (Graham)	.02	.01	.03	
Peanut butter	−.03	−.05	.14	−.07
Rice	.02	.03	.0	−.09
Salad and cooking oil	−.02	−.11	−.02	−.06
Salad dressing	−.01	−.105	−.03	−.14
Syrup	−.01	−.01	.01	−.05
Desserts	.0	.02	.03	−.17
Dessert pies	.0	.07	.09	
Dessert topping	.01	−.045	.02	−.16
Gelatine desserts	.0	.025	−.075	−.17
Laundry and cleaning products	.0	−.05	.0	−.035
Laundry detergents	−.03	−.055	−.065	−.11
Liquid detergents	.01	−.035	.0	−.03
Miscellaneous dry laundry aids	−.02	−.11	.025	.17
Miscellaneous dry cleaning aids	−.03	−.04	.02	−.04
Other	.03	−.07	−.08	−.01
Paper products	.02	−.005	−.025	−.04
Cleansing tissue	.02	−.02	.01	−.065
Food wrappers	.03	.025	.05	.14
Napkins	−.05	.22	.0	
Toilet tissue	.03	.015	−.05	−.075
Towels	−.01	−.03	−.025	−.025
Waxed paper	.02	−.07	−.02	−.05

Summary

Mean prices paid by blacks and by whites in stores of various affiliations for brands of several products were compared. Generally, prices paid in chain stores by whites in the suburb, whites in the outer city, and blacks in the inner city were similar. However, whites in the outer city paid relatively more than whites in the suburbs for beverages, packaged goods, and laundry and cleaning products purchased in independent stores. Inner city blacks purchasing in independent stores paid more than outer city whites for beverages, desserts, packaged goods, laundry and cleaning products, and paper products.

4

Food Prices in Chicago: 1969

The study reported in this chapter is based on entirely different kinds of price data than were employed in the study described in the last chapter, and so furnishes a useful perspective on both methodology and findings. In addition, this investigation covers a more recent time period—1969.

The Data

During the period January 20 through February 15, 1969, 108 grocery stores in Chicago and in towns outside of Chicago were visited and prices collected for several products. The study was organized by the Task Force on Public Aid of the Church Federation of Greater Chicago in order to provide information for the state welfare allowances (96). The surveyors were volunteers from the The Cook County Department of Public Aid, church groups, and other similar organizations. Each surveyor selected the dates of his visits and, presumably, the stores he visited. Included in this study are prices collected for the least expensive available brands of each of thirty-two products. For each product, a package size was specified (occasionally a small range, such as 6 to 7 ounces), but if that size were unavailable, the surveyor was instructed to select the most economical size and record both its price and size. All the surveyors were admonished to explain to the store manager what they were doing and to take their time in completing the price questionnaire.

Disadvantages

There are several possible sources of bias in these data. The chief one perhaps is the length of the time interval during which the prices were gathered. During that three-and-one-half weeks, the book prices might have changed so that some stores of a given chain may have

35

been using one set of prices, other stores of the same chain, another set. In viewing these data, then, one must implicitly assume one of two hypotheses. The first is that the book prices for each chain did not substantially change during the time period or that all store visits were made during the same (and shorter than three-and-one-half weeks) period. (This is perhaps not implausible given normal tendencies to procrastinate.) The second is that the number of stores of a given chain visited during a given week were proportionately the same for all areas surveyed.

The selection of the store or stores by the volunteer himself may have tended to cause stores either relatively good or bad in appearance to be overrepresented in the same sample since the volunteer may have tended to visit the store he usually shopped at or a store he suspected of high prices. But if the stated chain policy regarding departures from the book prices is true, such selection should cause no bias (unless competitive pressure or tendency of products to spoil is related to store appearance). The brands chosen, as noted, were the cheapest available; but since stores of the same chain should have the same cheapest brand and the bulk of the analysis below treats each chain separately, no bias should result from that selection method.

Because the surveyors were inexperienced (and possibly biased regarding the study's conclusions), reporting errors may have been made. In fact, either because the item was out of stock or through error, prices for package sizes other than those specified were reported although no pattern appeared in the mean numbers of such entries by chain and area. There was a tendency for stores in Chicago to be surveyed proportionately more by Department of Public Aid workers while stores in the suburbs were generally visited by church group volunteers.

These data were analyzed by the Church Federation, and the conclusion was reached that "food prices are definitely higher in inner city areas than in outer city or suburban areas" (96). The author feels a reanalysis of these data is necessary and informative for two main reasons. First, in the Church Federation analysis, only a market basket was examined, but some food items or groups of items may have prices higher in the suburbs, others, prices higher in the inner city. Such differences, if they exist, cannot be seen in the market basket (and, in fact, can offset each other), but may provide clues to chain store pricing policies. Second, the results of the

Church Federation analysis were presented very casually—no measures of statistical significance were given.

Analysis

The data were analyzed in this study by calculating the mean prices charged per standard unit (ounce or pound) by stores of a particular chain in each of four geographical areas: "Far Suburb," "Near Suburb," "Outer City," and "Inner City."[a] The towns further than approximately twenty miles from Chicago comprised the Far Suburb area; towns closer than twenty miles, the Near Suburb area. The Outer City area consisted of community areas of Chicago that were chiefly in the north and northwest sections of the city. The Inner City area was composed primarily of community areas where 25 percent or more of the residents were nonwhite. Four chains with stores in all four areas were examined. Also, all other chains were considered together in the "other" category.

Mean prices were computed for each of thirty-two products as well as for a market basket of these products that corresponded to approximately 80 percent (by weight) of the weekly food needs of a family of four (see Appendix for the weights used for each item). Moreover, for each of seven product groups, partial market baskets were formed by weighting the mean price charged for each product in the group by its market basket weight and summing. These partial market baskets summarize the results for groups of products.

Findings

Some variation in the prices collected was expected due to recording errors and the length of the survey period. As noted earlier, during the three-and-one-half weeks when the prices were gathered, the book prices might have changed so that some stores might have been using one set of prices, other stores of the same chain which were visited later, another set. Although this situation produced noise in the data, it is not likely that it caused bias since there is no reason to believe that the distribution of store visits over the survey period

---

[a]The "Near Suburb" area corresponds to the "Suburb" area in Chapter 3; "Outer City" and "Inner City" areas are the same in both Chapters 3 and 4.

differed among areas. Any remaining price variation should be due to price decreases because of competitive pressures or danger of spoilage. If such variation were found to differ among areas, that finding might support the allegations of consumer groups that sales are more plentiful in suburban and outer city stores.

The equality of price variances among areas was examined with the aid of Bartlett's test (which is based on the Chi-square statistic). For A & P, Jewel, and "other" chain stores, 32 of 85 comparisons led to variance differences significant at the .10 level or higher. (National and Kroger stores were not analyzed this way due to insufficient sample sizes.) Price variations were relatively largest for produce, margarine, and chicken wings, products that frequently appear in store promotions.

A relative lack of variation in the prices of Inner City stores is consonant with, but not necessarily indicative of relatively fewer sales in that area. In A & P stores, for only 6 of 29 products was the coefficient of variation (standard deviation/mean) largest in the Inner City; while for Jewel stores, in 14 of 24 cases, it was largest in the Inner City. For "other" chains, price variation was highest in the Inner City for 23 of 32 products, but that possibly reflects a greater variety of small chains in that area.

Initially analysis of variance was employed to examine differences among the price means. Of the 125 comparisons among areas for all the chain categories, significant differences (.10 level) were found for only 21 (one would expect 12.5 by chance alone). However, several of these analyses of variance are suspect due to the inequality of variances discussed above.

A more appropriate test for price differences consists of t-tests between the mean prices in neighboring areas for each product and chain (Table 4-1). Only for National stores between Outer and Inner City was the number of such price differences that were statistically significant (10) much greater than the number expected by chance (3.2) and that result may be due to the sample size—just one Inner City National store was surveyed. In sum, the differences in mean prices among areas were not, *overall* statistically significant.

The most striking aspect of the detailed results in Table 4-1 are the differences among the prices for many products in stores of the same chain. Some of these differences may have been due to book price changes during the time interval of the survey or due to reporting errors, but their preponderance and magnitudes are startling in view of the announced chain pricing policy. Moreover, upon inspection some patterns emerge in these differences.

Far Suburb versus Near Suburb

Interestingly, in three of the chains the Far Suburb residents were charged more for the market basket than were the Near Suburb residents—perhaps due to higher transportation costs. A & P charged less in the Far Suburb area for fruits, but showed no patterns for any of the other product groups. Prices in National stores were higher in the Far Suburbs than the Near Suburbs for canned goods and dairy goods. Jewel appeared to have charged higher prices for meat and vegetables in its Far Suburban stores. Canned goods and dairy goods in Kroger stores were cheaper in the Far Suburbs, fruits more expensive. In stores of "other" chains, dairy goods and fruits were generally less costly in the Far Suburbs; vegetables and miscellaneous goods more costly. No systematic patterns for the prices of staple goods were observed for any of the chains. Those products that were consistently higher priced in the Far Suburb area, without regard to chain, were American cheese, bacon, bologna, and lettuce; lower priced products were canned peas, eggs, and apples.

Near Suburb versus Outer City

In three of four chain categories, Outer City residents were charged more than Near Suburban residents. A & P appeared to have charged more in the Outer City than in the Near Suburbs for canned goods and meat, but generally less in the Outer City for dairy goods and staple goods. National charged more for fruits in the Outer City, but less for staple goods there. Jewel and Kroger also charged more for fruits in the Outer City. Canned goods and vegetables in Kroger, though, were less costly in the Outer City area than in the Near Suburb area—while staple goods in Kroger were more costly in the Outer City area. The "other" chain category, however, showed the most pronounced patterns of prices–higher prices in the Outer City for canned goods, meat, and miscellaneous goods. Products more costly in the Near Suburbs than in the Outer City consisted of canned peas and flour; less costly, tuna, lard, bananas, ground beef, and cornmeal.

Table 4-1
Relative Price Differences by Product

Item	Far Suburb Price – Near Suburb Price Far Suburb Price					Near Suburb Price – Outer City Price Near Suburb Price					Outer City Price – Inner City Price Outer City Price				
	A & P	National	Jewel	Kroger	Other	A & P	National	Jewel	Kroger	Other	A & P	National	Jewel	Kroger	Other
Market basket	.03	.01	.04[b]	*	-.01	-.06	.0	-.01	*	-.09[a]	.04	-.09	*	.14	-.03
Canned goods:															
Grapefruit juice	-.02	.04	-.06	-.12	.04	-.86	.0	.0	.04	-.17[b]	.46	-.08[a]	.03	-.07	-.05
Peaches	-.03	.01	.01	-.62[b]	-.03	-.11	.0	.07	.29	-.04	.10	-.71[b]	-.22	.13	-.02
Peas	-.15	.03	-.05	-.17	-.07	.01	.07	.11	.09	-.10	.31	.09	-.09	.06	-.07
Tomatoes	.29	-.01	.30	-.29	.02	-.36	.09	-.03	.11	-.26[c]	-.11	.02	-.37	.13	-.04
Tuna fish	.09	.15	.01	-.03	-.07	-.15	-.01	-.15[c]	.19	-.02	.07	-.12	-.08	-.06	-.04
Group	.10	.04	.0	-.26	.0	-.45	.01	.01	.15	-.12	.31	.19	-.08	.01	-.04
Dairy goods:															
American cheese	.23	-.13	.04	.02	.0	-.32	.06	-.05	-.15	.02	.02	-.05	.04	.07	.07
Eggs	-.09	.06[c]	-.13	-.09	-.01	.04	-.01	.03	.07	-.03	.12	-.16	.04	.01	.01
Lard	.0	.07[c]	.02	-.98[c]	-.09	.0	-.03	-.04[b]	-.22[b]	-.02	-.04	.03	-.17	.0	-.03
Margarine	-.22	.38[b]	.01	-1.70	-.03	.04	.02	-.02	.46	.06	.39[c]	.13	-.04	.09	-.22
Milk	-.03	.03	-.03	-.08	.01	.10	-.03	.04	-.05	-.02	-.15	-.05	-.03	.09[a]	-.03[a]
Group	-.04	.09	-.03	-.21	.0	.05	-.02	.02	.03	-.11	.0	-.04	-.03	.08	-.04
Fruit:															
Apples	-.50[b]	-.12	-.21	.64	-.09	.43[b]	-.06	-.11	-1.78	.03	-.62[b]	.46[c]	.04	.44	-.17
Bananas	-.07	.02	.05	.09	-.12	-.10	-.02	-.05	-.15	-.07	-.19	.0	.0	-.04	.12
Group	-.34	-.05	-.09	.05	-.10	.29	-.04	-.09	-.89	-.01	-.43	-.26	.03	.38	.42
Meat:															
Bacon	.15	.12	.19[a]	.0	-.07	-.05	.06	-.23[a]	.0	.0	-.02	.10	-.07	.0	-.09
Bologna	-.03	.01	.11	.38	.10	-.28	-.09	.02	.09	-.03	.39	.08	-.34[c]	-.03	-.11
Chicken wings	-.39	-.10[c]	.15	.0	-.18	.32	-.08[c]	-.12	.0	-.05	-.25	.09	-.50	.61	-.19
Ground beef	.03	-.02	-.05	.0	.03	-.03	-.11[b]	.0	-.03	-.10	.0	.20	-.04	.03	.04
Hot dogs	-.25	.09	.06	-.17[a]	-.10	-.03	.03	-.05	.10	.06	.18	-.16	-.03	.05	-.02
Group	-.15	-.01	.07	.30	-.04	.08	-.06	-.08	-.40	-.06	.04	-.07	-.20	.21	-.07

Staple goods:															
Bread	-.10	-.04	.03	.0	.0	.01	.07	.09	-.40	-.05	.12[c]	-.48[b]	-.06	.29	-.02
Coffee	.0	-.11	-.01	.22	.0	-.05	.03	-.01	-.26	.03	-.06	-.11[c]	-.07	.18	-.03
Flour	-.05	.04[b]	-.03	-.11	-.01	.05	.12[c]	.11	.06	.04	.0	-.59[b]	-.14	-.07	-.08
Sugar	.0	.01[b]	.03	-.01	.02	.01	.00	-.04	-.01	-.05[c]	.03	.0	.0	.03	-.02
Group	-.07	-.03	.02	.02	.0	.01	.04	.07	-.29	-.03	.08	-.41	-.06	.22	-.03
Vegetables:															
Cabbage	-.34	-1.15	.29	.11	.06	.49	.24	-.03	.15	.05[b]	-.56	.32	.18	-.31	.0
Lettuce	.17	.02	.22	-.16	.09	-.07	-.05	.08	.23	-.19[b]	.0	.22	.16	.10	.09
Potatoes	-.25	.04	.15	-.25[a]	.11	.21	.05	-.04	.10	-.16	.0	.08	.03	-.11	.03
Group	-.21	-.23	.22	-.09	.09	.29	.11	-.06	.14	-.08	-.17	.10	.10	-.15	.03
Miscellaneous:															
Chocolate pudding	-.06	-.03	-.01	.0	.0	.05	-.06	.04	.0	-.11[c]	.08	-.01	-.19	.10	-.08
Cornmeal	.27	.07	-.05	.23	.11	-.36	.05	-.11	-.29	-.06	.04	-.13	.02	.0	-.01
Instant milk	-.03	.03	-.03	-.08	.01	.10	-.03	.04	-.05	-.02	-.15	-.05	-.03[a]	.09	-.03
Maple syrup	-.18	.01	-.08	.20	-.15[c]	.03	.13[b]	.15	-.13	-.02	.11	-.51[b]	-.06	-.11	.08
Oatmeal	.01	-.07	.05	-.16	.19[c]	-.01	.09	-.05	.14	-.23[b]	.04	-.34[a]	.19	.0	.03
Peanut butter	.09	-.28[c]	.03	-.03	-.03[b]	-.05	.04	-.06[c]	.03	-.10	.21	.39[a]	-.06	.25	.03
Rice	-.03	-.01	.17	-.20[b]	.20[b]	-.09	-.03	-.17[c]	.12	-.14[c]	.03	-.78[a]	.05	.0	.01[b]
Spaghetti	.13	-.13	-.05	.13	.05	-.16	.20	.01	-.20	-.05	.16[c]	-.50	-.19	-.04	-.15[b]
Group	.24	-.06	-.01	-.05	.05	-.04	.06	.00	.05	-.06	.10	-.18	-.01	.03	.02

*No observations.

[a]Significant at .01 level.

[b]Significant at .05 level.

[c]Significant at .10 level.

Outer City versus Inner City

Only National and "other" chain stores charged more for the market basket in the Inner City than in the Outer City. A & P consistently charged less for canned goods and miscellaneous goods in the Inner City area and more only for fruits. National did charge more there for staple goods and miscellaneous goods but less for fruit and meat. Canned goods, meat, and staple goods were higher priced in the Inner City in Jewel stores and vegetables lower priced. Dairy goods, meat, and staple goods were generally less costly in Kroger Inner City stores. Canned goods, meat, and staple goods, though, were consistently higher priced in "other" chain stores in the Inner City area and only vegetables were lower priced there. Products that were consistently higher priced in the Inner City were tuna, milk; lower priced were American cheese, eggs, ground beef, lettuce, oatmeal, and peanut butter.

Summary

These price findings can be summarized loosely as follows: Generally, city residents were charged more than suburban (particularly near suburban) residents, especially for fruits and meats. Regarding comparisons between the outer city and inner city, no general conclusions seem possible—for certain products, prices were higher in inner city stores; for others, lower.

Appendix

Weekly food requirements for a family of four, prepared by Miss Jacqui Alberts, a nutritionist at Mile Square Health Center, from a week's list of menus sent her by the Illinois Department of Public Aid when she requested the precise list of items used in determining the welfare allowance for food (96). Items marked with an asterisk were not included in this study.

3 cans grapefruit juice (46 oz.)
1 can tomatoes (16 oz.)
1 can green beans* (15½-17 oz.)
1 can peas (15½-17 oz.)
1 can tuna fish (6½-7 oz.)
2 cans evaporated milk* (13 oz.)
12 oz. peanut butter (2/3 of 18 oz. jar)
2 cans peaches (29-30 oz.)
12 oz. maple syrup (½ 24 oz. jar)
8 large loaves white bread (20-24 oz.)
1 3-4 oz. pkg. chocolate pudding
5 qts instant nonfat dry milk
16 oz. cornmeal (2/3 of 24 oz. or 1/5 of 5 lb.)
24 oz. oatmeal (4/7 of 42 oz. pkg.)
8 oz. grits* (1/3 of 24 oz. pkg.)
2 oz. rice (1/8 of 1 lb. pkg.)
4 oz. spaghetti (1/4 of 1 lb. pkg.)
2 lbs. navy beans* (dried)
3 lbs. flour (3/5 of 5 lb. sack)
2 lbs. sugar (2/5 of 5 lb. sack)
½ lb. brown sugar* (½ of 1 lb. box)
½ lb. coffee (½ of 1 lb. can)
1 box salt* (26 oz.)
1 small tin pepper*
1 box raisins* (15 oz.)
4 gallons white milk
½ lb. American cheese (½ of 1 lb. box)
1¾ doz. eggs
3 lbs. margarine

1 lb. lard
1 lb. hot dogs
2½ lbs. chicken wings
1½ lb ground beef
8 oz. bologna
¼ lb. bacon (¼ of 1 lb. pkg.)
1 lemon*
2 bags carrots* (2 lbs.)
1 head lettuce
4 lbs. cabbage
2 lbs. apples
1 lb. onions*
2 lbs. bananas
10 lbs. potatoes

5

The Demand Side: Grocery Shoppers

Linking the prices stores charge and the prices families pay is shopping behavior: the stores frequented, the brands preferred, and package sizes bought. Underlying all these consumer choices is the amount of effort invested in shopping. Some people buy the first item they see or shop at the store closest to them; others spend considerable time and effort searching before they make a purchase. On the average, the shopper who shops around will pay lower prices for a given item.

The effort a shopper exerts depends on the value of the product sought, the shopper's expectations regarding purchase opportunities, and the transportation and time costs of shopping. For illustration, a person will spend more time shopping for a house than for a six-pack of beer. In some areas, a person will shop more if he has a readily available car than if he must rely solely on public transportation.

The extent to which the families comprising a grocer's market shop around governs in large measure the prices he can charge. The shopping habits of a store's customers define the set of competitors for that store. As an extreme case, consider a single store in a neighborhood of families who will not or cannot go to stores outside that neighborhood. That store will enjoy a monopoly, at least until another store moves nearby. The real-life case is more complex—the residents of a neighborhood will exhibit varying tendencies to shop. Moreover, even a specific family may exert varying amounts of search effort depending on the day of the week or the time of the day. However, in general one can say that a grocery store will enjoy relatively more short-run monopoly power as a relatively larger proportion of his potential customers tend not to shop around, other things being equal.

This chapter discusses models of shopping behavior which spotlight the key factors determining search effort. Next, the relevance of such models to inner city areas is evaluated by surveying previous empirical work and by analyzing data from the panel employed in the findings of Chapter 3.

45

Models of Shopping Behavior

A sequential search is simply a search procedure consisting of several stages; at any stage, a decision can be made either to halt the search and use the current alternative or to continue the search in an attempt to secure a better alternative. Examples of such situations include: someone buying a used car, a truck driver looking for a gasoline station, a shopper buying instant coffee, and a purchasing agent looking for a supplier. The basic problem in a sequential search is to develop a decision rule indicating when the search should be stopped. For a special case of sequential search, this problem has been solved by Becker (110) and Stigler (147). For somewhat more general versions of the problem, solution approaches have been suggested by Howard (127) and Morris (133). This section surveys those sequential search situations pertinent to a family buying groceries. A formal mathematical treatment of these cases can be found in the unpublished paper "The Utility of Search" (144).

Persistent and Transitory Opportunities

A basic distinction among search situations is between those with *persistent* opportunities and those with *transitory* opportunities. For example, when one is examining prices on coffee packages in a single supermarket, the prices found are persistent opportunities—when the search is completed, the coffee can be bought at any of the prices discovered during the search. That situation is quite different from the one faced by an investor who wishes to buy a particular stock. The prices of the stock at different points in time are transitory opportunities—if the search is terminated, the investor must buy the stock at the last quoted price, not at the lowest of all the prices he has observed.

Shopping among grocery stores does include elements of both the persistent and transitory opportunity situations. Within a store the opportunities (prices) are all available whenever the purchase decision is made. However, if a shopper does not make a purchase but moves to another store to search for the product, the prices found at the first store are attainable only at the cost of returning to that first store. Analytically, this persistent/transitory situation is tedious to solve formally, but it does suggest some interesting hypotheses about shopping behavior that are described later in the chapter.

Decision Rule

The general solution to a search problem typically has the following form:

Suppose $n - 1$ searches have been made.
Continue to search as long as:

$$V_n > C_n$$

Where: V_n = Expected value of nth search, and

C_n = Expected cost of nth search.

For example, suppose one wants to buy a large box of brand X laundry detergent and is now in a store where the price of that box is $2. Further suppose that one knows of another store selling that same brand and package size for $1. However, to go to that store will cost $.50 in bus fare and two hours of time valued at $.75 an hour. In such an illustration, the value of going to the other store would be the difference between the two prices, $1. The transportation and time costs of going to that other store would total $2. Since the value is less than the cost, the trip to that other store would not be made. On the other hand, if the trip to the other store required only 30 minutes, the visit would be made.

In reality the situation would involve uncertainties. Most likely one would not know for sure the price of the item in the other store, but would have some idea of the probability that the store was charging $1, or $2, or $3, etc. Also the time and money costs to get to the other store may be uncertain. That is why the decision rule given above is phrased in terms of *expected* values.

The most difficult part of making the general decision rule operational for a specific case is the derivation of an expression for the value of the nth search, V_n.

Value of Search

The value of the nth search is basically the difference between what one has now (for instance, a price of $2.) and what one might expect to get by further searching (say, a price of $1.). Its exact form depends firstly on whether persistent or transitory opportunities are being considered. If the opportunities are persistent (say, several brands of detergent at one store), then what one now has in hand is the *best* of all previously inspected opportunities (that is, the best buy of all brands already examined). If the opportunities are transitory (just one kind of detergent in a store), then what one has now is the *last* observed of all previously examined opportunities.

The monetary value of the nth search is directly related to the magnitude of the purchase. For example, the more detergent one is buying or the relatively more expensive the brand desired, the more worthwhile it is to shop around.

Finally, the value of further searching depends on the perceived differences in price and quality between successive opportunities. If one feels that all stores charge similar prices for the same goods, there is little incentive for shopping around. If one feels that prices of detergents vary considerably among stores (detergent is a loss leader), then, in general, shopping is more worthwhile.

Cost of Search

Search costs, C_n, have two components: transportation charges and the opportunity cost of time. Bus fares, taxi rates, and, for car-owning families, gasoline and upkeep are examples of transportation costs. Less obvious but equally important is the value a shopper sets on his or her own time. Sometimes the value of time can be directly determined—when a woman with many children must hire a babysitter, for example. In other cases, the opportunity cost of time may be less clear. Shopping may displace work or leisure time and one can only guess at how an individual would value such a loss. For example, perhaps the opportunity cost of time may be less for salaried than for hourly-paid employees since typically the former have more flexible work schedules.

Shopping Patterns

Overall, the analysis of search models (see 144) suggest several patterns in shopping behavior, including the following:

A consumer can be expected to search relatively more, other things equal:

1. the relatively larger the quantity of product to be bought;

2. the relatively more expensive the product;

3. the relatively more products to be purchased;

4. the relatively more price sensitive the shopper is;

5. the relatively wider the distribution of price and quality among opportunities is *perceived* to be;

6. the relatively less experienced the shopper is (or the relatively less frequently he purchases the commodity);

7. the lower the transportation cost of moving to another store;

8. the lower the time cost of moving to another store; and

9. the relatively lower the shopper's marginal opportunity cost of time.

Hypotheses 1, 2, and 3 concern the amount purchased. Hypotheses 4, 5, and 6 pertain to the shopper's knowledge of the market (that is, his or her shopping ability). The remaining observations relate to the relative cost of making a trip to a store.

Characteristics of Inner City Families

The hypotheses suggested by search models provide a framework for understanding the shopping habits of families in various neighborhoods. The findings below come from a variety of sources.

Amounts Purchased

Several studies indicate that black consumers spend less per grocery store transaction than do consumers in other demographic groups (50, 140, 159). For example, Table 5-1 displays findings from a 1967 study in Cleveland based primarily on an eight-week panel of 500 families and depth interviews with 125 of them (138). All demographic groups except "black" consisted of white families.

Black families may tend to buy smaller quantities of individual food items than white families because they lack freezer, refrigerator, or other storage space, cannot amass money for one large weekly shopping trip, or for some commodities wish to avoid the depletion of large stores of food by children in search of snacks (65).

Table 5-1
Average Size of Transaction by Demographic Group

	Black	Blue Collar	Young Married	High Income	Small Town	All
Average expenditure per transaction ($)	4.88	7.44	5.85	6.87	6.75	6.42
Average number of items per transaction	12.9	15.3	13.7	14.2	16.3	14.2

Source: *Progressive Grocer. Consumer Dynamics in the Super Market.* New York: Progressive Grocer, 1966.

According to Herman Smith, board chairman of Jet Foods, a black-owned-and-operated food store chain, "The black shopper's reason for not buying multiple units isn't because of lack of money, but more likely because of lack of space at home to store the goods" (138).

To the extent that search effort depends on the quantity of products that consumers plan to purchase on a single shopping trip, blacks may be expected to search relatively less than whites, other things being equal.

Perceptions of Price and Quality Distributions

Studies that have investigated consumers' perceptions of the price levels in grocery stores include Progressive Grocer (138), Oxenfeldt (135), and Brown (114). Brown examined one thousand housewives and twenty-seven supermarkets in five cities. He found that housewives tended to form their price images of stores from the same cues. For example, extra services, in their minds, were positively associated with higher prices, larger sales volumes with lower prices. Brown concluded that misperceptions (misrankings) were most likely to occur where the alternative stores were most similar and most numerous.

The relevant issue here, however, is not the number of erroneous price perceptions (except in the long run when, say, the housewife who continously errs may not trust herself), but whether the perceptions are biased high or low and whether these biases are related to race of shopper. No study directly pertaining to that question is known to the author.

What indirect evidence there is appears to be somewhat contra-
dictory . In a study focused only on low-income black families,
Goodman observed that, "shoppers' perception of the relative level
of prices of different stores are generally good, not only as between
stores of different types but also among stores of a given type" (71).
In possible contrast, the Real Estate Research Corporation reported
that low-income consumers do not shop prices to the extent higher
income consumers do (140).

This last finding is weakly corroborated by studies attempting to
determine the criteria shoppers use to select stores. For the general
population, the most important criteria in food store selection
appear to be the store's reputation concerning price level and quality
of food (118). A sample of black housewives, on the other hand,
produced a quite different ordering: convenience of location and
friendly atmosphere were found most important; low prices least
important (138).

However, a lower emphasis on price as a shopping criterion may
reflect the relative lack of spatial mobility among blacks, rather than
ignorance of prices. For example, King and De Manche found that
among low-income families, store location and access to public
transportation was more important to blacks than to whites (128).
But in a study of nonfood shopping where both department stores
and discount houses might be expected to be similar distances from
the shoppers, a larger proportion of blacks than whites were found to
frequent discount houses—behavior consistent with an interest in and
a knowledge of prices (125).

One finding of the President's Committee on Consumer Interests
was that "the panel believes that there is already substantial evidence
that most poor people do not possess the necessary knowledge, skill,
and time to get full value for their dollars" (100). While there
appears to be very little empirical evidence as to whether the price
and quality perceptions of black (or low-income) and white (or
high-income) shoppers do, in fact, differ, there is one sense in which
the statement by the Committee on Consumer Interests may be true:
to the extent black families send children to the grocery store more
than do white families, the average shopping ability of the black
family (not the individual adults) may be less than that of the white
family. The empirical evidence pertinent to such a comparison is also
limited although the *Detroit Free Press* claimed that:

Their [black families'] financial and dietary problems are further compounded by the common practice of sending children down to the store for an evening to fetch a bag of stuff for dinner. This isn't from laziness. Many of the Inner City mothers are supporting children without a father, and after a day of hard work they are in no mood to cope with the store. (57)

Costs of Shopping

The cost of shopping to a family depends on such factors as the number and ages of the children, whether or not the housewife is working and, if so, the type of job (for instance, part-time or full-time), the family income, and the availability of automobiles or public transportation. For example, a housewife responsible for several young children cannot shop at many stores unless a friend, relative, or babysitter minds the children at home. A housewife who does not have access to a car or convenient public transportation may find it difficult or costly to make major shopping trips at grocery stores several blocks from her home.

Table 5-2 compares statistics for white and black families in the *Tribune* panel (described in Chapter 3) that are relevant to the cost

Table 5-2
Selected Demographics for White and Black Panel Families (November/ December, 1960)

	White	*Black*
Number of households	1023	223
Average number of persons per household	3.5	3.9
Average number of persons who are 16 or over and not in the labor force per household	1.0	1.0
Average income per household	$7500	$6000
Percentage of households with one or more cars	75	50
Percentage of households with two or more cars	8	3
Percentage of households where housewife works	20	25

of searching among stores. The largest difference between these two sets of statistics corresponds to the percentage of households with one or more cars. A 1967 study of low-income families in Chicago similarly found that, of a sample of 365 families, 48 percent had cars (140).

Automobiles play a key role in grocery shopping (Table 5-3). Goodman, whose study may have examined somehwat lower income families than the ones covered by the Cleveland study, found that 45 percent of the families in a low-income section of Philadelphia used an automobile while shopping, 14 percent traveled by public transportation, and the rest walked (71). Of families with annual incomes above $5000, he found that 60 percent used cars while shopping; in the income class $2000 or below, 25 percent of the families drove to the grocery store.

Table 5-3
Means of Transportation while Shopping for Food

	Black	Blue Collar	Young Married	High Income	Small Town
Percentage who shop by car	77	76	97	100	100
Percentage who shop on foot	18	22	3	0	0
Percentage who shop by public transportation	5	2	0	0	0

Source: *Progressive Grocer. Consumer Dynamics in the Super Market.* New York: Progressive Grocer, 1966.

Supermarkets are typically less common in inner city areas. In fact, in 1969, supermarkets, superettes, and small stores all were relatively more numerous in the outer city areas of Chicago (Table 5-4). Such configurations of stores suggest that the relative lack of automobiles among black families leads to relatively high shopping costs for many inner city families.

Food Shopping Habits[a]

Although there has been much previous research concerning the behavior of black and low-income food shoppers (112, 115, 128),

[a]Sections reprinted with permission of the *Journal of Retailing.*

Table 5-4
Relative Numbers of Grocery Stores in Chicago

	Per Thousand Households		
Outer City Communities	*1964*	*1967*	*1969*
Supermarkets	.52	.51	.40
Superettes	.85	.54	.44
Small stores	1.90	1.72	1.44
Inner City Communities			
Supermarkets	.38	.37	.34
Superettes	.64	.83	.33
Small stores	2.14	1.84	1.26

Source: *Chicago Sun-Times/Daily News. Grocery Store Route List, City of Chicago and Suburbs, 1966 Edition.* Chicago: *Chicago Sun-Times/Daily News,* 1966. Also 1968, 1970, and 1972 editions.

generally these attempts have failed to compare the shopping habits of inner city residents with those of shoppers in other areas. The absence of comparable information concerning more affluent shoppers makes it difficult to evaluate the policy implications of such findings. Other shortcomings of previous work are methodological. In particular, all previously published studies have been based on questionnaire data. The accuracy of such data is limited to that of the respondents' memories. While recall data may be expected to be reasonably accurate for some questions (for example, stores usually patronized), responses to questions concerning details such as brands and package sizes purchased and behavior patterns over long periods of time must be viewed with some reservations. Finally, several of the previously reported studies have been based on sample sizes most observers would consider small—100, 50, or even fewer respondents.

The Data

The findings reported in this section are based on the panel described in Chapter 3. It consisted of over 1,100 families in the Greater Chicago Area. Available for each family were its reported purchases of twenty-two products during all of 1960 and three products during a two-and-one-half year span, 1963-66 (130,000 records altogether). The bulk of the discussion concerns the data base of twenty-two

Table 5-5
Products in Product Groups

Product Group	Product
Beverages	Soft drinks
Packaged goods	Cereal
	Coffee creamer
	Peanut butter
	Salad and cooking oil
	Salad dressing
	Saltine crackers
	Syrup
Desserts	Dessert pies
	Dessert toppings
	Gelatine desserts
Laundry and cleaning products	Laundry detergents
	Liquid detergents
	Miscellaneous dry cleaning aids
	Miscellaneous dry laundry aids
Paper products	Cleansing tissue
	Food wrappers
	Napkins
	Toilet tissue
	Towels
	Waxed paper

products since they are varied (Table 5-5). Findings for the other three products (close substitutes—regular coffee, instant coffee, and tea) are described later in order to provide a time perspective.

The sample size of this data base is sufficiently large to allow comparisons of the purchase habits of families classified simultaneously by area of residence, race, and income. Moreover, these data provide a detailed picture of purchasing behavior over a relatively long time span: an entire year. These features represent distinct methodological advantages over previous work.

One reservation to this study concerns the representativeness of families who participate in panels. The black families in this panel appeared to be more literate and have somewhat higher incomes on the average than did black families in Chicago in 1960 (see Chapter 3). Overall, the panel lacked families with male heads younger than twenty-six. Finally, panel families are generally more likely to be sensitive to prices than the population at large. The total impact may be to bias the findings of this study upward with respect to the spatial mobility of the shoppers.

A second reservation to these findings concerns their currency. Findings based on 1960 data may not hold for the 70s. This possibility was investigated by comparing the results for the twenty-two-product data (1960) to findings for the three-product data (1963-65) and to findings for a narrow group of products reported in a recently published study of Cleveland made during 1969 and 1970 (119). There were some differences (described at the end of this section), but in the main the purchase patterns found for 1960 were similar to those found with smaller data bases during the later years.

Characteristics of Families Examined

The families were first classified by area of residence: "Suburb," "Outer City," "Mixed City," and "Inner City." The definitions of the Suburb, Outer City, and Inner City areas are identical to those given in Chapters 3 and 4. The Mixed City areas consist of all areas in the city that were not classified as Outer or as Inner City areas. Generally, the mixed neighborhoods were geographically located between areas that were predominantly white or predominantly black. In addition to area of residence, families were classified by race and by income class (low—below $4,000; middle—$4,000-$8,000; high—above $8,000).

The Suburban panel families had a much higher mean income than families elsewhere (Table 5-6). Fewer than 13 percent of the Suburban families were in the low-income class as compared with roughly 25 percent of the families in the Outer City and nearly 50 percent for those in the Inner City. The low-income families tended to be smaller and to have older male heads and fewer full-time workers than the middle and high-income families, suggesting these families tended more to be composed of retired persons. The relatively high proportion of Inner City area housewives who worked is of particular relevance to this investigation, since employment constrains one's ability to shop around. Interestingly, the proportion of working wives was about the same for each income class in the Suburban area, but among whites in the Outer City and Mixed City areas the proportion was by far the largest for the high-income groups. Among blacks, though, sizable proportions of wives in middle-income families worked. Lack of a male head was not a factor

Table 5-6
Characteristics of Panel Families

| | | Area of Residence and Race | | | |
| | Suburb | Outer City | Mixed City | | Inner City |
Race	(White)	(White)	White	Black	(Black)
Number of families	370	441	147	131	62
Mean number of persons	3.8	3.5	3.4	4.0	3.3
Mean age of male head	46.6	49.4	47.0	45.5	53.1
Mean family income	$9,200	$7,500	$7,500	$7,300	$6,300
Mean number employed full-time	1.0	1.0	1.0	1.2	1.0
Percentage of families with employed wife	18	23	16	24	32

explaining whether wives worked or not—only two families had no male head.

Degree of Shopping Activity

To compare the degree to which residents of the various areas "shopped around," shopping matrixes were calculated for each product and for families in each area (121). Table 5-7 shows one such matrix. Notice that the 63 percent of the Suburban families who during 1960 purchased only one or two different brands at only one or two different stores might be considered "nonshoppers," while the 11 percent who purchased more than two brands at more than two stores might be called "shoppers." Families who bought more than two brands at one or two stores might be referred to as "brand-shoppers," and those who bought one or two brands at more

Table 5-7
Shopping Matrix for Suburb Area Purchasers of Soft Drinks (Percentages)

| | Number of Brands Bought | |
Number of Stores Visited	1 or 2	More than 2
1 or 2	63	21
More than 2	5	11

than two stores as "store-shoppers." While these labels may be criticized as being somewhat arbitrary, they do manage to capture the pattern of the data more than would, say, the mean number of brands purchased or the mean number of stores visited.

The proportion of nonshoppers among Inner City families appeared relatively large across all product groups (Table 5-8). Furthermore, on the average, Inner City families visited fewer different stores and purchased fewer different brands than families in other areas. This result was likely due to the relatively lower mobility of blacks due to the high proportion of black wives who work and the relative lack of automobiles.

Table 5-8
Median Percentages of Various Shopper Types

				Area of Residence and Race		
Product Group	Shopper Type	Suburb (White)	Outer City (White)	Mixed City White	Mixed City Black	Inner City (Black)
Beverages						
	Non-shopper	63	58	46	56	84
	Brand shopper	21	25	20	26	0
	Store shopper	5	7	11	9	5
	Shopper	11	10	23	9	11
Packaged goods						
	Non-shopper	69	74	74	71	83
	Brand shopper	14	10	10	16	9
	Store shopper	6	6	4	3	4
	Shopper	11	10	11	8	8
Desserts						
	Non-shopper	53	53	49	79	80
	Brand shopper	25	18	28	13	10
	Store shopper	7	6	0	7	3
	Shopper	10	23	15	6	12
Laundry and cleaning products						
	Non-shopper	54.5	51.5	58.5	74.5	68
	Brand shopper	17	15.5	22	5.5	0
	Store shopper	6.5	12.5	8.5	15	17.5
	Shopper	20	16.5	16	10.5	3.5
Paper Products						
	Non-shopper	66	60	66	62.5	77
	Brand shopper	10	12.5	8	6.5	5
	Store shopper	9.5	10.5	13.5	12	9
	Shopper	16.5	19	20	17.5	9.5

Generally, blacks were not as likely to be brand-shoppers as were whites, possibly reflecting some blacks' greater interest in certain national brands (142). With respect to the percentages of store-shoppers and shoppers, no systematic patterns emerged. As one might expect, there was a tendency for higher income families to have visited more different stores and to have purchased more different brands.

Stores Where Purchases Made

In this and following discussions, many of the findings are presented by giving median values over all the products in a given product group. Generally, the median represented quite well the results for the individual products. Where there was much variation among the products in a group, the variation is discussed in detail.

The stability of Suburban families' store preferences over all product groups is quite striking (Table 5-9). This stability may reflect making one or two major shopping trips to the same store week after week. The similarity of the percentages of the group for Inner City shoppers may indicate similar behavior. Outer and Mixed City residents appear to shop in a more fragmented fashion. For example, the portion of their purchases made at small independent stores—Mom 'n Pop stores—was larger for soft drinks than for any other product group.

Generally, the Outer City and Inner City residents appeared to frequent chain stores relatively more than did residents of the other areas. The whites' behavior may be explained by the relatively high density of chain stores in their area (Table 5-4). The shopping pattern of the blacks may be explained by the reverse—a lack of chain stores in the Inner City area that forces black families seeking low prices to travel when shopping. Given that one must travel to shop, one might as well go to a chain store rather than to a Mom 'n Pop store. Between blacks and whites in the Mixed City area, there were no systematic differences over all product groups. Among residents of all areas, there appeared to be a trend for the proportion of purchases made at chain stores to increase with income class, as one might expect because of higher spatial mobility of high-income families.

Table 5-9
Median Percentages[a] of Shopping Trips Made to Stores of Various Affiliations

			Area of Residence and Race			
Product Group	Store Affiliation[b]	Suburb (White)	Outer City (White)	Mixed City White	Black	Inner City (Black)
Beverages						
	Chain	65	44	49	37	63
	Aff. Ind.	16	18	6	12	7
	Unaff. Ind.	17	36	44	49	27
Packaged goods						
	Chain	65	75	54	65	68
	Aff. Ind.	16	16	6	13	17
	Unaff. Ind.	16	8	35	15	11
Desserts						
	Chain	65	73	65	58	79
	Aff. Ind.	16	16	14	27	14
	Unaff. Ind.	18	9	23	10	13
Laundry and cleaning products						
	Chain	66	68.5	60	57.5	69
	Aff. Ind.	16	19	15	17	13
	Unaff. Ind.	18	9.5	28	14.5	11
Paper products						
	Chain	62.5	73	65.5	69	69
	Aff. Ind.	17.5	16.5	8.5	10.5	12
	Unaff. Ind.	17	9	22.5	15.5	15

[a]Percentages do not sum to 100 since they are medians across all products in a group.

[b]Aff. Ind. is affiliated independent; Unaff. Ind. is unaffiliated independent.

Brands Purchased

Systematic differences in the percentages of private brands purchased were confined mainly to beverages and paper products (Table 5-10). Suburban families bought private brands of soft drinks relatively much more often than did other shoppers. Although that is consistent with the fact that Suburban families generally purchased soft drinks at chain stores—the type of store where private brands may be most common, it contrasts with the infrequent private brand purchases of the black city shoppers who also typically bought soft

Table 5-10
Median Percentages of Private Brands Purchased[a]

Product Group	Suburb (White)	Outer City (White)	Mixed City White	Mixed City Black	Inner City (Black)
Beverages	8.9	1.6	.6	1.3	1.0
Packaged goods	11.5	10.0	8.5	14.5	10.0
Desserts	5.0	6.0	2.0	6.5	7.5
Laundry and cleaning products	5.0	4.0	6.0	8.0	3.0
Paper products	6.5	7.5	1.5	1.0	.0

[a]Excluding products where private brands comprise less than 1% of total sales.

drinks at chain stores. A similar contrast holds for paper products. Both may be explained by a relative lack of private labels in the Mixed City and Inner City areas or, possibly, by a preference for national brands by shoppers in those areas.

Weekday when Shopping Trip Made

A slightly higher proportion of Suburban residents' shopping trips were made on Thursday, Friday, or Saturday than were those of shoppers in other areas (Table 5-11). This finding perhaps reflects the role of the family car in suburban food shopping: during the week the car may not be available. The days blacks shopped did not appear to differ consistently from those whites shopped. However, there was

Table 5-11
Median Percentages of Purchases Made on Thursday, Friday, or Saturday

Product Group	Suburb (White)	Outer City (White)	Mixed City White	Mixed City Black	Inner City (Black)
Beverages	68	62	66	51	64
Packaged goods	70	63	69	68	61
Desserts	68	63	64	62	71
Laundry and cleaning products	70.5	65	67.5	63.5	62.5
Paper products	70	66	68.5	70	69

a quite pronounced trend, overall, for higher income families to be more likely to shop on Thursday, Friday, or Saturday. That would be consistent with the need of low-income families to purchase small amounts of food frequently to avoid the high inventory costs that accompany major shopping trips.

Average Size of Package Purchased

Across all product groups, a slight pattern appeared with respect to average size of package purchased (Table 5-12). For beverages, Suburban shoppers bought larger bottles on the average, in line with their interest in economy as shown by their tendency to buy private labels of soft drinks. Inner City residents did buy, on the average, smaller packages of all products studied except paper products.

Other Time Periods

Three-Product Data (1963-66). The findings for 1963-66 (Table 5-13) generally echo the above observations. No overall pattern was found for private brand purchases. Relatively more whites than blacks were found to be "shoppers." However, smaller average package sizes were found for blacks, probably reflecting their relatively lower *per capita* usage rates for coffee products during the mid 60s. Whites and blacks in the mixed city area did appear to

Table 5-12
Median Rank[a] with Respect to Average Package Size Purchased

| | Area of Residence and Race | | | | |
Product Group	Suburb (White)	Outer City (White)	Mixed City White	Black	Inner City (Black)
Beverages	1	2	3	4	5
Packaged goods	2	3	5	1	4
Desserts	2	3	2	3	4
Laundry and cleaning products	2.5	3	2	3	5
Paper products	3	3	3	5	1.5

[a]Rank among five demographic groups for a given product group: 1–largest, 5–smallest.

Table 5-13
Selected Findings from Three-Product (1963-66) Data Set

Finding	Product	*Suburb (White)*	*Outer City (White)*	*Mixed City White*	*Black*	*Inner City (Black)*
				Area of Residence and Race		
Percentage of shopping trips made to chains	Coffee	67	67	73	71	63
	Instant coffee	76	72	62	64	69
	Tea	68	76	76	79	65
Private brands as percentage of purchases	Coffee	18	23	18	12	26
	Instant coffee	9	9	6	22	34
	Tea	16	21	12	12	5
Rank with respect to average package size	Coffee	2	3	1	5	4
	Instant coffee	2	1	3	5	4
	Tea	1	2	3	4	5
Percentage of nonshoppers	Coffee	12	9	14	24	14
	Instant coffee	47	47	48	65	45
	Tea	32	38	34	37	61
Percentage shoppers	Coffee	67	67	77	49	49
	Instant coffee	28	24	19	18	20
	Tea	37	35	39	19	13

frequent chains relatively more often in 1963-66 than in 1960, possibly because of increases in mobility.

Cleveland Study (1969-70). During 1969 and 1970, the Department of Agriculture studied food retailing in low- and high-income areas of the Cleveland Standard Metropolitan Statistical Area. Part of the study focused on purchase habits as reported during personal interviews with 318 homemakers. The percentages of shopping trips by type of store were not investigated, but respondents were asked the primary store at which they shopped. For both high- and low-income areas, chain store mentions were positively correlated with family income. National and private brand purchases for six products were discussed: no systematic difference across all products was found. The average package size for three of four products examined were larger in the low-income area, but these differences "appeared to be traceable to differences in family size" between the two areas (119). In sum, for aspects on which there is comparable data, results of the 1969-70 study were consistent with the patterns observed in 1960.

Determinants of Shopping Effort

An attempt was made to examine the effects on search effort of factors besides race and income and to obtain more precise estimates of their relative contribution. The rationale underlying this work was the basic hypothesis that those consumers who search relatively more should, on the average, pay relatively lower prices, other things being equal.

The methodology consisted of performing cross-section regressions across families purchasing selected products. The dependent variable in these regressions was mean price paid per unit measure (ounce or pound). The independent variables fell into two classes, those related to search effort and those related to market structure.

Search Effort

s_1 = Product expenditure as proportion of family income.

s_2 = Number of responsible (age sixteen and over) family members not in labor force.

s_3 = Family annual income in thousands of dollars.

s_4 = Number of cars owned by family.

s_5 = Average size of package purchased.

s_6 = Average size of purchase.

s_7 = Sum of sizes of all purchases by family over time interval studied.

s_8 = Occupation of family head classified as "salaried" or "hourly paid"; 0 if salaried, 1 if hourly paid.

s_9 = Number of persons in family.

s_{10} = Age of family head in years.

Market Structure

x_1 = Race of family; 0 if white, 1 if black.

x_2 = Area of residence; 0 if suburb, 1 if city.

x_3, x_4 = Racial composition of area of residence; (1,0) if white, (0,1) if black, (0,0) if mixed.

The data base for these regressions once again consisted of panel data from the Chicago *Tribune*. For stationary samples of approximately 600 greater Chicago families, data for three products during a one-year interval (1960) and three products over a two-and-one-half-year span (beginning in October 1963) were examined.

Product Prices

Initially, the mean prices paid for *products* were examined (Table 5-14). Pairwise correlations between the independent variables were uniformly low, most below .20, excepting those between average size of package, s_5, and average size of purchase, s_6. For that reason, the sum of all sizes purchased over time, s_7, was tried as an alternate for average purchase size. The correlations with average package size were lower, but the results did not markedly differ so they are not shown.

The R^2 values are all highly significant due to the large sample sizes. The more important aspect of these results, however, are the signs of the regression coefficients. Those signs corresponding to number of responsible family members not in labor force confirm

Table 5-14
Results of Regressions across All Families Who Purchased a Given Product (Expected Signs in Parentheses)

Product	Number of Familes	(−) s_2	(+) s_3	(−) s_5	(−) s_6	(+) s_8	Market Structure Variable (+) x_1	R^2
			Search Variables					
Rice	533	−	+[b]	−[a]	−[b]	+	+[a]	.50[a]
Regular coffee	459	−[b]	+	−	+	−[c]	−[a]	.08[a]
Instant coffee	317	+	+	−[a]	+	−	−	.58[a]
Tea	486	−[a]	+	−[a]	−	−	−[b]	.18[a]
Gelatin desserts	652	−[c]	+	−[a]	−[a]	−	−[b]	.27[a]
Cleansing tissue	536	−	*	−[a]	−[b]	−	+[a]	.11[a]

[a]Significant at .01 level.

[b]Significant at .05 level.

[c]Significant at .10 level.

*Contributed less than .0001 to R^2.

the search model as do those for the income variable, although less strongly. One difficulty in interpreting the income variable coefficients concerns the possible differences in type of product searched for by families of differing income. Higher income families may be searching for different commodities (that is, name brands) than lower income families. Although the signs of the average size and average purchase size variables also generally support the search model, their interpretation is also ambiguous due to the tendency of manufacturers to charge lower unit prices for larger packages. The signs for the occupation variable contradict the search model, but this variable was an admittedly weak measure of marginal earnings foregone.

In these initial regressions, race was the only variable explicitly meant to account for market structure. In four of six cases, its sign was negative, but it will be shown below that these results simply reflect differences in brand preferences and do not contradict charges that blacks pay more for food.

Brand Prices

The ambiguity of certain of the product regression findings suggested the need for a more thorough job of controlling for brand and store chain preferences, and for market structure. Such a detailed analysis was performed on three products (coffee, rice, and laundry detergent). For each, regressions were run across all purchases of a particular *brand* in stores of a particular affiliation (Table 5-15). Brand C for coffee and rice were leading private brands; all other brands studied were leading national or regional brands. Besides the additional market structure variables, the independent variables in these regressions included proportion of family income accounted for by total expenditures on product and number of cars owned. Omitted were average package size due to multicollinearity and the occupation variable due to its apparent crudeness.

The race and area of residence variables (x_1 and x_3) appeared to be relatively highly correlated (between $-.48$ and $-.92$) but both were felt sufficiently important to be retained in these stepwise regressions. Among the remaining pairs of variables, there were a few cases of correlation near .6, but these instances were not felt to be sufficiently numerous or systematic to cause the deletion of any variables.

The regression coefficients for the first four search variables (product expenditure as proportion of income, number of responsible family members not in labor force, income, and number of cars owned) had disappointingly low T-ratios—only 16 of 96 were above 1.64. In 17 of 24 brand/store categories, the sign of the product expenditure variable was in disagreement with the search model. The signs for the number of responsible family members and income variables did not display any consistent patterns. The signs of the variable for number of cars owned, however, did display a systematic pattern consonant with search theory—in 18 of 24 categories, the sign was negative. The coefficients for the average package size variable tended to be highly significant and in 23 of 24 categories, they had negative sign. But, as discussed earlier, these strong results may reflect quantity discounts more than differential search effort.

The findings for the market structure variables overall appeared stronger. Note particularly that the coefficients for the race variable were consistently positive (19 of 24 categories), suggesting that, for these three products, blacks paid more for a given brand purchased in a store of given affiliation.

In sum, the search model was not validated by these brand/store category regressions. That failure is not surprising given the character of frequently purchased products—relatively low monetary outlay, purchase with other products, impact of advertising and dealing, and price differences linked to area. Market basket data would likely promise a larger chance of empirical success. However, these regression results did generally confirm the price findings reported in Chapter 3.

Summary

This chapter explored differences and similarities in shopping behavior. The major findings were: The proportion of nonshoppers among inner-city area families was relatively large for all product groups. While outer-city and mixed-city area shoppers appeared to fragment their shopping trips—buying different products in stores of different affiliations, suburban and inner-city area shoppers seemed

Table 5-15
Results of Regressions Across All Families Who Purchased a Given Brand in a Given Store Category (Expected Signs in Parentheses)

| Product | Store Category | Brand | Number of Families | Search Variables | | | | | Market Structure Variables | | | | R^2 | F |
				s_1 (−)	s_2 (−)	s_3 (+)	s_4 (−)	s_5 (−)	x_1 (+)	x_2 (+)	x_3 (−)	x_4 (+)		
Rice	A & P	A	96	+[b]	−	+	−	−[a]	+	−	−	+	.38[a]	7.52[a]
	Nat'l.	A	217	+[b]	−	+	−	−[a]	+[b]	+	+	+	.22[a]	7.74[a]
	Jewel	A	228	+[a]	−[b]	+[b]	−	−[a]	+	+[c]	+	−	.33[a]	13.60[a]
	Certified	A	212	+	+	−	+	−[a]	+[c]	+	−	+	.40[a]	17.19[a]
	Indep.	A	168	+[b]	−	−	+	−[a]	+	+	+	−	.38[a]	12.17[a]
	A & P	B	38	−	+	+	−[c]	−[c]	−	−[a]	−	−	.77[a]	2.22[a]
	Jewel	B	91	+	+	−	−	−[a]	+[c]	+	+	+[b]	.32[a]	5.67[a]
	Certified	B	90	+[a]	−[c]	+	−	−[a]	−	+[b]	+	+[b]	.39[a]	7.31[a]
	Indep.	B	53	+[b]	−	−	−	−[a]	+	+	+	+	.46[a]	5.86[a]
	Jewel	C	172	+[b]	−	+	−	−	−	+	+	−	.00	.68
Regular coffee	A & P	A	68	−	+	−	+	−	+	−	+	+	.01	1.06
	Nat'l.	A	59	−	−	+	−	+	+	−	−	−	.00	.45
	Jewel	A	143	+	+[c]	+	+	−[a]	+[c]	−	+	−	.26[a]	6.69[a]
	Certified	A	67	−	+[c]	+	−	−[c]	+	−	+	+	.03	1.24
	Indep.	A	123	−	+	+	−	−[a]	+	+	+	−	.18[a]	3.89[a]
	A & P	C	72	+	+	+	−	−[a]	+	+	−	−[c]	.21[a]	3.16[a]

Laundry detergent													
A & P	A	95	−	−[b]	−	−	−[a]	+	+	+	.24[a]	4.20[a]
Nat'l.	A	115	+	−	+	+	−[a]	−	−[b]	+	.00	1.02
Jewel	A	126	+	−[c]	−	−	−[a]	−	+	+	.10[b]	2.39[b]
Certified	A	93	−	+	−	−	−[a]	+[b]	−[b]	+	.20[b]	3.65[a]
Indep.	A	149	+	+	−	−	−[a]	+[b]	+[b]	+	.25[a]	6.58[a]
A & P	B	68	+	−	+[c]	−	−[a]	+	+	−	.25[a]	3.53[a]
Certified	B	53	+	+[b]	−	−	−[a]	+	+	−	.36[a]	4.22[a]
Indep.	B	85	+	+[b]	+	−	−[c]	+	+[a]	−	.25[a]	4.11[a]

[a]Significant at .01 level.

[b]Significant at .05 level.

[c]Significant at .10 level.

to confine their purchases of all products chiefly to a particular class of store. Moreover, inner-city area shoppers shopped at chain stores generally for about the same proportion of their purchases as outer-city area shoppers and as suburban shoppers. Finally, for beverages and paper products, blacks bought proportionately fewer private brands; for other product groups, no systematic differences emerged.

Some of the inner-city area shoppers, with few quality, low-priced stores nearby, apparently felt forced to travel to find chain stores. [This finding has been confirmed by other studies such as (71).] The mixed-city area shoppers, surrounded by more chain stores and not having to exert themselves so much, ended up making relatively fewer purchases at chain stores and as a group possibly paid more for groceries than did the inner-city area shoppers.

6

The Supply Side: Grocery
Stores

The last chapter has shown that there may be economic pressures restricting the mobility of shoppers, namely time and money costs of going to stores. Especially among low-income families these forces may act to curtail the shopping choices available to them. Such a situation may be reflected on the supply side by limited and short-run monopoly power for grocers, which means de facto price discrimination since higher prices may be charged for given items in certain areas. Such power is limited by competition from other stores since there is a point when a store's prices become too far out of line and shoppers will pay the cost (say, hire a taxi) of going to a store in another neighborhood. Such power would be short-run since there are no major entry barriers in grocery retailing.

This chapter presents a microeconomic view of the ghetto grocery store. Operating cost and gross margin information are examined. Finally, changes in the numbers of food stores in Chicago from 1959 through 1971 are traced to determine those neighborhoods that have been relatively the most profitable for grocers.

The Underlying Model

Figure 6-1 describes the relative economic situations for the same food store newly placed in either of two areas. For simplicity, assume the store sells just one type of grocery product—say a specific brand of coffee. Suppose that the distribution of competing stores (location and price) is the same in both areas.

If the shoppers in area 1 are in general more mobile than those in area 2 (because they own cars, have fewer children, etc.), then the market demand curve in area 2 will be higher at all points than the market demand curve in area 1. That occurs because the price of coffee purchased in other stores is cheaper to area 1 residents due to their greater mobility. That is, to the area 1 shoppers the available substitutes are relatively more attractive than they are to the less mobile area 2 shoppers.

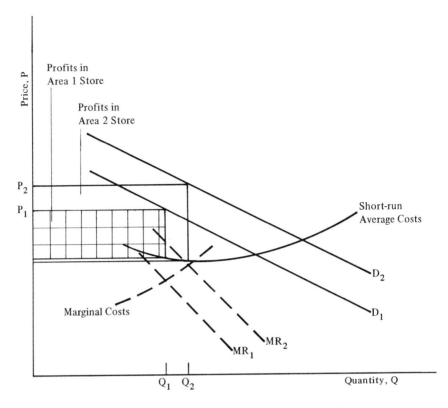

Figure 6-1 Monopoly Profits of Grocery Store

D_i = Demand curve in area i.
MR_i = Marginal revenue curve in area i.
P_i = Price in area i.
Q_i = Quantity sold in area i.

Note: Profits = (Price − Average Cost) · (Quantity)

Under the assumption of identical cost curves in both areas, the area 2 store will then enjoy short-run monopoly profits that are larger than those enjoyed by the area 1 store.

Now suppose that the short-run average cost curve is everywhere higher in area 2 than in area 1. Then the monopoly profits of the area 2 store would be reduced. Whether they are larger or smaller than those of the area 1 store will depend on the difference in the height and shape of the cost curves.

Operating Costs

The most comprehensive studies of food retail costs are those compiled by Earle and Sheehan (4) and by Holdren (158). However, these sources do not provide breakdowns by neighborhoods and so can serve only as a general background to an examination of the relative costs in various geographical areas. The area-by-area cost figures given below come primarily from the National Food Commission, the trade press, and interviews with men in the retail food industry, such as chain store executives.

Costs in National Food Chains

Land cost or rent, payroll expense, inventory shrinkage (pilferage), and insurance are the cost categories the variations in which are most commonly cited in studies or articles as the explanation for price variations. Table 6-1, based on chains throughout the United States,

Table 6-1
Selected Operating Ratios for Chains in the United States, 1961-65

Item	1961	1962-63	1963-64	1964-65
Number of chains	51	52	67	58
Average sales per store ($000)	1227	1319	1327	1392
		Percentage of Sales		
Gross margin	21.76	22.13	22.23	22.48
Expense				
payroll	10.13	10.14	10.19	10.30
insurance	.38	.42	.44	.44
property rentals	1.67	1.76	1.80	1.82
total interest	.76	.81	.78	.75
unclassified	.89	1.13	.76	.67
Total expense	20.54	21.13	21.11	21.28
Net operating profit	1.22	1.00	1.12	1.20
		Percentage of Net Worth		
Pre-tax earnings	23.22	21.89	22.96	23.21
After-tax earnings	11.25	10.74	11.51	12.33

Source: Earle, Wendell and John Sheehan. *Operating Results of Food Chains, 1964-65.* Ithaca, N.Y.: Cornell University Press, 1966.

provides a perspective of the relative importance of these cost categories in the balance sheet of a food store. These results can be summarized: for chains, gross margin, the difference between sales and cost of goods sold, was typically about 22 percent of sales, payroll expense a bit more than 10 percent, insurance expense around .4 percent, property rental near 1.75 percent, unclassified expense (which may include inventory shrinkage) in the vicinity of 1 percent, total expense approximately 21 percent, and net operating profit slightly more than 1 percent.

Costs in Chain Stores versus Costs in Independent Stores

Most of the available cost information concern chains only. For certain types of costs, the costs incurred by independents may be greater than those incurred by chains. In particular, independents may lack purchasing, warehousing, and transportation economies of scale enjoyed by the chains and so may have lower gross margins as shown in Table 6-2. As Holdren (158) observed, "chain prices are lower in part because of real distribution cost saving . . .," although he noted that the chain's buying and distribution advantage is not "overwhelming."

To the extent that independent stores, especially the smaller stores remain open longer than chain stores, their payroll expense may be higher. That this is not revealed by Table 6-2 probably reflects independent grocers' employment of family members whose wages are unreported or are understated. Land costs or rent may be

Table 6-2
Means of Selected Operating Ratios for Stores in Portland, Maine, and Topeka, Kansas (Percentage of Sales) by Affiliation, 1964-65

Item	Chain	Chain	Independent	Independent	Discounters	All
Gross margin	21.3	19.6	18.6	16.1	15.7	19.0
Labor expense	10.2	9.7	8.1	7.6	6.6	8.8
Total expense	21.0	18.1	18.3	15.4	15.2	18.0
Net profit	.3	1.5	.3	.7	.5	1.0

Source: National Commission on Food Marketing, *Organization and Competition in Food Retailing, Technical Study No. 7.* Washington, D.C.: Government Printing Office, June 1966, p. 328.

relatively less among independent stores to the extent they are less likely to have parking lots than chain stores.

Variations in Operating Costs among Areas

Paralleling the findings reported in previous chapters, the discussion below compares operating costs between suburb and city and, within the city, between black and white areas and between low- and high-income areas. The time period discussed are the 60s—the time interval for which price data were analyzed.

Suburb and City. Grocery stores in the city may have higher land costs and lower transportation costs than those in the suburbs.

For example, the real estate manager for one of the leading chains in Chicago provided the following rough comparison of 1969 land costs in Chicago:

Area	Size of Plot (including store and parking lot)	Cost of Plot	Cost per Sq. Ft.
City	70-75,000 sq. ft.	$300-400,000	$7
Suburb	120-160,000 sq. ft.	$150-400,000	$2

There also may be difficulties just in assembling a packet of land in the city sufficiently large on which to build a supermarket. Property taxes also may be higher in the city.

For orders of the same quantity, transportation costs appear somewhat higher to suburban stores. For example, in 1969 one Chicago food warehouse was charging 1 percent on deliveries made within 25 miles; 1¼ percent on deliveries made between 25 and 50 miles.

Miscellaneous expenses that may be higher in the city than in the suburbs include the theft of shopping carts. According to Partch (161), carts (which in 1969 cost about $35 each) stolen in the city are usually lost—converted into wagons or barbecues; more of those taken by suburbanites are retrievable.

Within the City—Black (Low-Income) and White (High-Income) Areas. Table 6-3 contrasts key operating ratios for stores in black and white areas; Table 6-4 provides similar information for Iowa and

Table 6-3

Means of Selected Operating Ratios for Stores in Two Midwestern Cities (Percentages of Sales) by Racial Composition of Neighborhood, 1963

	City A Mean of 2 Chains		City B Mean of 3 Chains	
Item	White	Nonwhite	White	Nonwhite
Annual sales ($000)	1407	952	1976	1331
Gross margin	19.9	20.6	18.7	18.7
Inventory shrinkage	.43	.44	.25	.32
Total expense	14.4	17.6	14.3	15.2
Net margin	4.50	3.00	4.40	3.60

Source: National Commission on Food Marketing, *Organization and Competition in Food Retailing, Technical Study No. 7.* Washington, D.C.: Government Printing Office, June 1966.

high-income areas. Although there are differences among the gross margins, such differences do not imply variations in operating costs. Gross margins depend in large measure on the mixture of products sold by a store. Black areas, for example, are referred to as "pork markets" and the relatively higher margin on soul foods is one factor that can result in higher gross margins for black neighborhood stores (177). The relationship between the types of products sold and gross margins is examined in the next section of this chapter.

A more direct measure of the differences in operating costs among areas is "total expense." On the average, total expenses incurred by nonwhite or low-income area chain stores offset anywhere from .3 percent to 3.2 percent more sales than in white or high-income area stores. In general such intracity differences have been attributed to differences in payroll expense, inventory shrinkage, and insurance.

Of these three cost categories, payroll expense (about 10 percent of a chain store's sales) seems most likely to account for the observed differences in total expense. Although unions may produce similar wage rates in chain stores throughout a city, payroll expense may differ among stores through differences in the ratio of employees to sales. Since the average transaction is smaller in black area stores (Chapter 5), for a given level of sales, stores in black areas typically require more check-out personnel than those in white areas.

Another reason payroll expense as a percentage of sales can vary concerns the administrative economies enjoyed by stores of certain size. Holdren (158) found average sales per worker to increase with annual store sales up to annual sales of $2 million (then leveling off,

Table 6-4

Means of Selected Operating Ratios for Stores in Two Midwestern Cities (Percentage of Sales) by Income of Census Tract, 1963

| | City A | | | | | | City B | | | | Both Cities | |
| | Chain 1 | | Chain 2 | | Chain 3 | | Chain 4 | | Chain 5 | | Average | |
Item	High	Low[a]	High	Low	High	Low	High	Low	High	Low	High	Low
Annual sales ($000)	1243	1417	1493	927	1401	1320	2401	1352	1559	1011		
Gross margin	18.9	20.2	21.2	20.1	18.0	18.1	19.5	20.0	18.3	18.4	19.2	19.4
Inventory shrinkage	.50	.50	.28	.60	.10	.20	.49	.90	.24	.30	.32	.50
Total expense	13.9	14.5	15.8	18.2	14.9	15.2	17.1	18.5	12.4	14.4	14.8	16.2
Net margin	5.00	5.74	3.53	-.50	3.1	2.9	2.4	1.5	5.9	4.0	3.99	2.73

Source: National Commission on Food Marketing, *Organization and Competition in Food Retailing, Technical Study No. 7*, Washington, D.C.: Government Printing Office, June 1966, p. 340.

[a]Low income areas defined as census tracts in lowest income quartile.

and declining for annual sales above $5 million). Similar economies of scale for independent stores have been found (138). The chain stores in the nonwhite and low-income neighborhoods on the average are smaller and therefore likely experience a relative lack of labor economies of scale.

Chains reputedly have difficulty in placing managers in inner city stores and on occasion must pay a "hazardous duty pay" to inner city store managers (50). To the extent that practice is frequent, it can explain some of the difference between outer and inner city payroll expense.

Smith, Chairman of black owned and operated Jet Foods, has made an observation also germane to managerial costs: "A major weakness that has existed on the part of grocery chains is that they have a policy of sending their worst and weakest help to black area stores, and writing the entire store off as a tax loss." (138) More generally, others have alleged that, "Productivity of employees in these [poverty area] neighborhoods is generally lower than in the suburban areas" (50). These charges raise a potentially valid issue, but one that was beyond the scope of this study.

Payrolls in inner city stores may be higher than those of their counterparts in the suburbs because of the employment of security guards. For example, the Better Business Bureau of Greater St. Louis found that four of ten stores interviewed in the poverty area of St. Louis employed a security guard. A store with annual sales of about $2.6 million has about 50 employees (according to the manager of one large supermarket), so the addition of one security guard might raise the payroll by 1/50th or 2 percent, that is, from about 10 percent of sales to about 10.2 percent.

Summarizing the differences in payroll expense is difficult since the data vary in type. However, some ceiling estimate is in order and the author's subjective estimate is that, at most, the typical total difference in payroll expense between outer and inner city areas is of the magnitude of 2 percent of sales.

Pilferring customers are estimated to account for about 35 percent of inventory shrinkage, employees and outsiders such as men servicing vending machines accounting for the rest (50, 152). Hard estimates of inventory shrinkage are difficult to come by. Those in Tables 6-3 and 6-4 are probably the most reliable.

The evidence regarding inventory shrinkage suggests that the difference between white and black areas or between high- and low-income areas is much less than the 1 percent figure often cited. In Tables 6-3 and 6-4, the *largest* amount by which black or low-income area chain stores exceed their white or high-income area counterpart is .41 percent of sales. In the light of those figures, the following statement by Smith seems only slightly exaggerated: "Customer pilferage in grocery stores is no higher in ghetto or Black areas of our cities, and is often less high, than in white and suburban areas" (68). However, there are opposite views such as that of Marcus (78): "Pilferage is an increasing problem for business in general, but to the ghetto merchant it represents a battle for survival." Similarly, in a 1966 survey of one hundred supermarket managers, seventy-two felt pilferage was higher than average in low-income neighborhoods (157).

In cities where riots have occurred, such as Los Angeles and Detroit, insurance rates for stores have reputedly increased by 300 percent or more (1, 53, 161). Since the late sixties, grocery store insurance rates in Chicago were equal due to the Fair Plan Law (stores that have difficulty obtaining insurance are assigned to companies that give them insurance at the standard rate). The impetus for this law must have stemmed from existing disparities in insurance rates probably accentuated by the riots.

In sum, a rough (and upwardly biased) estimate of the difference in operating costs between chain stores in the outer and inner city is 3 percent of sales (Table 6-5).

For independents, the estimate may be somewhat higher, say, roughly 4 percent. In the chain comparisons, purchasing economies of scale were similar for stores of the same chain. To the extent inner city independents are relatively smaller, they do not enjoy purchasing economies of scale. Moreover, several sources note that many suppliers are reluctant to deliver in the inner city except during certain daylight hours, which may raise delivery costs to inner city stores, particularly the smaller independents.

Table 6-5
Estimated Cost Differences (Percentage of Sales)

Between:	Chains	Independents
Suburb and Outer City	−6	−6
Outer City and Inner City	−3	−4

Gross Margins

The gross margin for a specific grocery product, say, a brand of frozen peas, is the difference between its retail price and its cost to the retailer—wholesale price and warehouse and delivery changes. The cost of goods sold, as has been noted, typically may be somewhat greater for stores relatively far from the distribution centers and for stores that order in smaller quantities. To enjoy delivery economies of scale is a primary reason some independent stores are affiliated (for instance, IGA stores).

The overall gross margin for a store is the sum of the gross margins for the products weighted by the proportion of store sales accounted for by each product. That is,

$$G = \sum_{i=1}^{n} g_i s_i$$

Where: G = Store gross margin.
g_i = Gross margin for product i.
s_i = Product i share of store sales.
n = Number of products sold by store.

The difference between gross margin and operating costs is the net margin—the profit a grocery store enjoys.

Even if two stores pay the same costs of goods sold and charge the same prices, their gross margins will likely differ because of differences in the mixture of products each store sells. In particular, Donaldson and Strangways observed that the "...purchasing patterns [of poor or black shoppers] enable the ghetto chain to earn higher gross margins, other things equal" (153). The evidence they used to support their hypothesis was incomplete. However, this section presents findings that do indicate their observation was correct, though the typical difference in gross margin appears to be not as large as they implied.

To determine how the gross margins of stores in different areas may vary according to the mix of products sold, one first needs to know the shares of those stores' overall sales corresponding to each product. Purchase data by store affiliation and neighborhood were available for the group of products comprising the price examinations in Chapter 3, but, unfortunately, even a group of twenty products is small relative to the approximately three hundred products frequently found in supermarkets. Therefore it was necessary to employ another data base to investigate the relationship between gross margin and products sold.

The Data

The necessary data were found in the report of a 1967 study of ten Kroger supermarkets of similar size (sales of $29,600/week), located in the Cleveland area (138). These ten stores consisted of two selected from each of five types of areas—neighborhoods comprised chiefly of one of the following socioeconomic classes: high-income, blue-collar, black, young-married, and small-town families. (Table 6-6 displays selected demographic characteristics.) In each store during each of two four-week periods, the sales of each of 268 products were audited.

Every year, *Chain Store Age* publishes the average gross margins for all products sold by a large sample of United States supermarkets (1). This information is not broken out by area (black versus white, or low-income versus high-income). Therefore, the analysis below ignores the possible differences in costs of goods sold and in prices between stores in black (low-income) and white (high-income) neighborhoods, a reasonable assumption given that all stores belong to the same chain. However, it should be stressed that this section is

Table 6-6
Means for Various Demographics: Five Types of Neighborhoods

	High Income	Blue Collar	Black	Young Married	Small Town	All
Household size	4.3	3.7	3.7	5.0	4.7	3.8
Age of wife	44	47	43	33	44	41
Occupation (%):						
White collar	70	19	20	49	37	54
Blue collar	24	66	70	50	52	40
Retired	6	15	10	1	11	6
Weekly income	$238	$138	$127	$155	$144	$179

Source: *Progressive Grocer. Consumer Dynamics in the Super Market.* New York: Progressive Grocer, 1966.

concerned solely with the effect of sales mix on gross margin and does ignore possible price differences.

Groceries and produce and meat are discussed separtely; then a store's overall margin is considered.

Groceries

The product of gross margin and share of store sales—the contribution of an item to the overall gross margin of a store—was calculated for each of the 207 grocery items in the Kroger study. For clarity and brevity, though, these item-by-item results have been grouped into the forty product classes listed in Table 6-7. The category "baking needs," for example, consists of eleven products: extracts and coloring, nuts, chocolate syrups, cocoa, baking chocolate, cocoanut, corn starch, maraschino cherries, marshmallow creme, yeast, and baking soda.

Groceries' contribution to store gross margin was smallest for black area stores, largest for the high-income area stores. Most of the 1.4 percent difference was due to the frozen food category—sales in high-income area stores included a relatively large proportion of frozen food products. There were other products contributing relatively more to the gross margins of the high-income area stores than to those in the black area: dairy products (primarily cheese and ice cream), baking needs (especially nuts and toppings), cereals, snacks, and desserts (particularly potato chips), household supplies, paper products, and pet foods.

Comparing all five neighborhood types, groceries' contribution to gross margin was also high in the small-town areas and somewhat low in the blue-collar areas. The reasons for these differences seemed plausible. For illustration: high-income area stores received relatively more of their gross margins from convenience products such as frozen foods and correspondingly less from items such as canned vegetables. In blue-collar areas, apparel accounted for a relatively large portion of store gross margin. The gross margin for black area stores depended relatively less on frozen foods, relatively more on canned goods such as milk and juices. Health and beauty aids contributed more to gross margin in the blue-collar, black, and young-married neighborhoods than in the high-income and small-town areas.

83

Produce and Meat

The Kroger study included sales data for produce and meat items, but gross margins were not available for individual produce and meat

Table 6-7
Contribution to Overall Gross Margin (Hundreths of a Percent)

Product Class	High Income	Blue Collar	Black	Young Married	Small Town	All
Foods						
Baby food	5	5	4	5	4	5
Baking mixes	22	20	27	21	31	26
Baking needs	22	11	12	12	15	18
Bread, rolls, and cakes	105	89	101	91	118	99
Candy and gum	27	27	31	23	37	30
Canned fish	12	8	12	8	9	10
Canned fruit	30	21	24	17	38	28
Canned juices	19	16	24	9	18	18
Canned meat	28	37	32	28	34	32
Canned vegetables	27	44	43	35	54	39
Cereals	31	21	21	31	30	26
Coffee	16	20	17	17	18	19
Condiments, pickles, etc.	81	66	74	76	78	76
Dairy products	207	195	192	165	196	193
Dried vegetables	7	5	7	6	6	7
Frozen foods	163	90	85	99	93	109
Jams, jellies, and spreads	25	15	25	22	25	23
Macaroni products	8	12	9	11	13	12
Milk, canned and dry	4	6	11	4	8	7
Salad dressings	11	11	10	10	12	11
Shortening and oils	4	11	12	8	10	9
Snacks and desserts	38	22	19	31	34	32
Soft drinks	56	37	52	57	61	53
Soup	11	10	6	11	12	11
Sugar	8	7	12	7	12	9
Tea	9	6	4	5	7	7
Wine, liquor, mixes	7	6	8	4	7	7
Miscellaneous foods	6	2	3	3	2	3
Nonfoods						
Apparel	6	47	23	22	33	21
Cigarettes, cigars, etc.	32	42	39	41	43	39
Health and beauth aids	70	80	81	84	61	71
Household supplies	56	54	39	53	49	51
Magazines and books	11	12	7	16	21	15
Paper products	51	32	36	40	37	39
Pet foods	27	13	17	19	28	20
Pet supplies	7	9	1	8	3	4
School and writing supplies	3	3	1	3	5	3
Soaps and detergents	41	43	43	46	42	43
Toys	3	8	3	10	6	3
Miscellaneous nonfoods	46	48	35	67	31	49
Total (%)	13.42	12.11	12.02	12.25	13.41	12.77

items. However, contributions to gross margins for these product categories could be approximated by using aggregate gross margins that were available for all produce items and for all meat items. In particular, the produce and meat sales shares for all but the black area stores were multiplied by the gross margins computed by *Chain Store Age* (produce–29.6 percent, meat–21.7 percent). Because the mix of meat and produce items was expected to be quite different in black area stores, the gross margins reported in the Donaldson-Strangways study (produce–31.1 percent, meat–27.5 percent) were used for these stores (153). However, the Donaldson-Strangways meat margin was undoubtedly high for the Kroger stores since pork accounted for only 34 percent of their meat sales as opposed to 55 percent of meat sales in the Atlanta poverty area chain Donaldson and Strangways investigated.

The estimated contribution of produce items to store gross margin was lowest for the black area stores (Table 6-8), primarily because produce's share of store sales was by far smallest in black area stores (Table 6-9). In stores in other areas of Cleveland produce accounted for a third more of all sales than in black area stores.

In contrast, meat sales in black area stores were 28.3 percent of store sales as compared to 23.8 percent in high-income areas, 26.2 percent in blue-collar areas, and 25.1 percent in young-married areas. This sizable difference in meat's share of sales as well as differences in specific meat items sold (more pork in black area stores) resulted in an estimated contribution to store gross margin from meat items that is considerably higher in black area stores than in stores elsewhere. Of course, the difference may be somewhat less great than shown in Table 6-8, since, as noted, the Donaldson-Strangways margins are likely biased high as estimates for Cleveland.

Table 6-8
Contributions to Overall Gross Margins

	High Income	Blue Collar	Black	Young Married	Small Town	All
Groceries	13.42	12.11	12.02	12.25	13.41	12.77
Produce	2.63	2.60	2.12	2.72	2.20	2.54
Meat	5.16	5.69	7.78	5.45	5.00	5.15
Overall	21.21	20.40	21.92	20.42	20.61	20.46

Table 6-9
Shares of Store Sales

	High Income	Blue Collar	Black	Young Married	Small Town	All
Groceries	67.0	64.7	64.9	65.4	69.3	67.4
Produce	9.2	9.1	6.8	9.5	7.7	8.9
Meat	23.8	26.2	28.3	25.1	23.0	23.7

All Products

So large is the estimated meat contribution to gross margin in black areas that it overpowers the relatively low contributions of groceries and produce and results in black area stores exhibiting the highest overall gross margin. The difference between the gross margin in the high-income area stores and the black-area stores is, however, only about .7 percent.

It is informative to compare that .7 percent with differences in gross margins estimated in other studies. The National Commission on Food Marketing (168) found, for various chains in various cities (Tables 6-3 and 6-4), gross margin differences between white or high-income areas and black or low-income areas ranging from −1.1 percent to 1.3 percent. When grocery and produce gross margins are combined with the figures Donaldson and Strangways reported (153), their study suggests the gross margin in poverty area stores is 3.3 percent above the average gross margin for United States chain stores. It would seem that the consensus figure is below 1 percent and that the Donaldson-Strangways finding reflects special conditions.

Relative Profitability

The previous sections on operating costs and on gross margins were meant to provide some insight into the internal economics of food stores. However, there are questions as to whether such data as were discussed can unequivocally resolve the issue of whether inner city grocery stores are relatively more profitable.

The operating cost data were averages across several stores and the gross margin data were based on the experience of several chains. While such information is important, it obscures the extremes—the stores incurring large losses or enjoying high profits. It is just those extreme cases, particularly the very profitable stores, in which one is interested if one is examining the possible existence of monopoly profits. Furthermore, if there are monopoly profits, one is interested in their duration. The data supporting the previous sections unfortunately were not time series data, and so conditions could not be examined over time.

Much of the information in the sections on operating cost and gross margin pertained to chains only. As was shown in Chapters 2 and 3, between area price differences were much more common and much larger among independent stores than among chain super-markets. The operating cost and gross margin figures discussed so far can be extrapolated to independent stores only with reservation and that is a major weakness.

Fortunately one can indirectly estimate the relative profitabilities of stores by examining the changes in their numbers over time. Suppose that at some point in time the grocery stores in a particular area were earning monopoly profits. If from then on demand remained constant and if there were no barriers to entry, eventually all food store monopoly profits would be removed as more stores entered the area.

In reality, an area is continuously in disequilibrium. Grocery demand changes as the number, sizes, and incomes of families change, causing the number of stores in an area to continually fluctuate. Such changes furnish a natural experiment for examining the relative profitabilities of urban food stores. An increase in the number of inner city food stores relative to the number of outer city food stores, after accounting for demand changes and assuming other things equal, would suggest inner city stores reap relatively larger profits; a relative decrease would imply relatively smaller profits.

The major reservations to such an analysis are the two main parts of the *ceteris paribus* assumption, namely that: (1) barriers to entry are the same everywhere, and (2) propensities to exit are the same everywhere. The data on which this section is based consist only of urban food stores: if they had included suburban areas, the assumption of an equal entry barrier might be suspect due to large property cost differentials between city and suburb. However, there appears to be no evidence to suggest the existence of a systematic difference in the degree of difficulty in opening food stores in various areas of most cities.

Regarding the propensity of store owners to close, one might argue that inner city retailers may be more reluctant to close since they have less attractive alternative uses for their capital. That argument, however, would be valid only if these retailers were restricted to the inner city—if they were black, for example, and discrimination kept them from white areas. However, much public comment has been addressed to the fact that many inner city retailers are white. To the extent that is so, inner city retailers might be *more* likely to leave the market than outer city retailers.

The Data

This investigation is focused on the city of Chicago for the period 1959 through 1971. The units of analysis are the seventy-five community areas which comprise Chicago and which have been briefly described before. These areas were first delineated more than forty years ago by the Social Science Research Committee of the University of Chicago. Their boundaries were drawn on the basis of several considerations including the growth and history of the area, local identification with the area, the local trade area, and barriers such as the Chicago River, railroad lines, roads, and parks (10). While the real-life boundaries of these communities may have changed to some extent over time, the initially defined boundaries have not been altered. These community areas thus provide an opportunity to study changes over time in fixed areas that in the main remain meaningful communities.

For each of the seventy-five community areas, the following data were available for various years: number of small food stores, number of superettes, number of supermarkets, number of families, average family size, average family income, average number of persons per dwelling unit, and number of persons classified by race.

The store data were obtained from the grocery store route lists of the *Chicago Sun Times/Daily News* (3). These data consist of the numbers of supermarkets, superettes, and small stores for each community area for the years 1959, 1964, 1967, 1969, and 1971. A grocery store route list contains the address and size class designation of *every* grocery store in Chicago and is used by, among others, the newspaper's advertising salesmen. Discussions with the marketing research manager of the *Sun Times/Daily News* convinced the author that these lists are highly accurate. In addition, the author is personally familiar with one Chicago area during the 1964-69 period and found the relevant route lists to be complete lists of the stores of various sizes in operation in that area for each year.

The demographic data on population, income, and so on consist of United States census data for 1950, 1960, and 1970, all on a community area basis (5, 10, 20). The only item missing was family income for 1970 which was not available at the time of this writing. However, income estimates for 1968 were available and these have been used (3). All dollar figures have been converted into 1960 dollars through the use of the consumer price index (16). Estimates of the demographic variables for the five years corresponding to the store data were developed separately for each of the seventy-five community areas by linear interpolation (or extrapolation for 1971) of the census data available for each area.

Methodology

The general model examined is expressed as follows:

$$\Delta S_{ijt} = f(\Delta I_{jt}, \Delta F_{jt}, \Delta S_{ujt}; B_{jt})$$

Where:

ΔS_{ijt} = Change in number of type i stores per family in community j between time $t-1$ and t.

ΔI_{jt} = Change in median family income in community j between time $t-1$ and t.

ΔF_{jt} = Change in average family size in community j between time $t-1$ and t.

ΔS_{ujt} = Change in number of type u stores per family in community j between time $t-1$ and t.

B_{jt} = Proportion of blacks in population of community j at time t.

The logic of the model is that any change in the number of stores per family in a given area depends on two basic types of variables: (1) variables related to demand changes; (2) variables related to differences in short-run monopoly profit. Demand for stores of a certain type can be expected to be linked to changes in income (that alter purchasing power) and changes in family size (that alter a family's needs for food). Demand for stores of a certain type also may change due to changes in shopping habits such as an increased preference for supermarkets. In short, changes in family income, family size, and stores of other types per family are expected to account for store changes due to demand changes.

The second type of variable—that linked to the profitability of the store—is the one of particular interest in this study. If grocery stores in outer and inner city areas face similar demand curves and have similar operating costs, then changes in the number of stores per family in outer and inner city areas should appear about the same once changes in income, family size, and the number of stores of other types have been considered. If not, the rates of change should differ. More specifically, if inner city stores are relatively more profitable, inner city stores should be increasing relative to outer city stores. The variable used to measure the degree to which a community was in the inner city is the proportion of blacks in the community. Other variables (described below) were also considered, but proportion of blacks appeared to be the most sensible choice.

The model was investigated primarily by ordinary least squares regressions made across seventy-four of the seventy-five community areas (the Loop—Chicago's downtown area—was omitted as atypical). Two basic regression models—linear and loglinear—were employed:

$$(1) \qquad (S_{ijt} - S_{ijt-1}) = \beta_1 + \beta_2 (I_{jt} - I_{jt-1}) + \beta_3 (F_{jt} - F_{jt-1})$$
$$+ \beta_4 (S_{ujt} - S_{ujt-1}) + \beta_5 (S_{vjt} - S_{vjt-1})$$
$$+ \beta_6 B_{jt} + \epsilon$$

$$(2) \qquad (S_{ijt}/S_{ijt-1}) = e^{\beta_1} (I_{jt}/I_{jt-1})^{\beta_2} (F_{jt}/F_{jt-1})^{\beta_3} (S_{ujt}/S_{ujt-1})^{\beta_4}$$
$$(S_{vjt}/S_{vjt-1})^{\beta_5} (B_{jt})^{\beta_6} e^{\epsilon}$$

Where: u and v represent types of stores other than type i.

ϵ = random disturbances

Variations of these models that did not include changes in other store types or which replaced the black proportion variable with dummy variables or with a variable representing the average number of persons per dwelling unit were also examined, but they were found to be less informative. In addition, interaction between income and family size was examined by including a term representing change in estimated food expenditures computed as a function of income and family size according to relations developed by a research firm in the course of studying retail sales in Chicago (139). Generally, little or no interaction effect was observed for either the linear or loglinear model.

Findings

Changes in numbers of stores per family were examined for the four intervals 1959-64, 1964-67, 1967-69, and 1969-71. Generally, the overall statistical strength of the linear models was much greater than that of the loglinear models and so the findings for the loglinear model are shown only for small stores (Table 6-10) for illustrative purposes. (The loglinear results for superettes and supermarkets are available on request.)

Each of the four periods suggests somewhat different conclusions regarding the hypothesis of higher profits for inner city small stores and superettes—the store types for which higher prices have been observed in the inner city (Tables 6-10 and 6-11). The period 1959-64, for example, appears to have been a time interval when small stores were being upgraded to or replaced by superettes. Moreover, there was no significant difference in changes in small stores or changes in superettes between communities with high or low proportions of blacks. Between 1964 and 1967, however, small stores and superettes per family were increasing in black areas relative to white areas at a statistically significant rate. Such a finding is consistent with higher monopoly profits in the inner city.

For the 1967-69 interval, however, small stores were decreasing in black areas relative to white areas at a statistically significant rate. It is doubtful, though, that this result can be attributed primarily to low profits in the inner city. Rather, much of this change may be due to the rioting and tensions that followed the death of Martin Luther King in April of 1968. Between 1967 and 1969, the number of small

Table 6-10
Regression Results: Changes in Small Stores per Family, 1959-71 (Standard Errors in Parentheses)

Model	Time Interval	Const.	Δ Inc.	Δ Family Size	Δ Supers	Δ Superettes	Black Prop.	R^2 2	F
Linear	59-64	.025	-.082[c] (.058)	.261 (.245)	-.235 (.198)	-.297[a] (.091)	.003 (.058)	.24[a]	4.29[a]
	64-67	-.046	.027[a] (.012)	.027 (.050)	-.357[c] (.287)	-.695[a] (.070)	.058[a] (.015)	.60[a]	20.60[a]
	67-69	-.034	.044[a] (.017)	.006 (.062)	-.412[c] (.318)	-.414[a] (.155)	-.054[a] (.013)	.32[a]	6.39[a]
	69-71	-.026	.016 (.015)	.020 (.049)	-.407[c] (.299)	-.946[a] (.126)	-.007 (.011)	.47[a]	11.92[a]
Loglinear	59-64	.485	-.055 (6.474)	-4.789 (11.965)	.060 (.066)	.010 (.074)	.003 (.025)	.02	.24
	64-67	-.049	.730 (.649)	.340 (1.175)	-.016 (.026)	-.058[a] (.018)	.007 (.007)	.16[b]	2.49[b]
	67-69	-.348	1.315 (4.224)	2.974 (7.754)	-.221[c] (.167)	-.037 (.109)	.021 (.033)	.001	.43
	67-71	-.085	.484 (2.776)	-.072 (5.700)	.102 (.405)	.182[a] (.049)	-.005 (.024)	.18[b]	2.92[b]

[a] .01 significance level.
[b] .05 significance level.
[c] .10 significance level.

Table 6-11
Regression Results: Changes in Superettes per Family, 1959-71 (Standard Errors in Parentheses)

Model	Time Interval	Const.	ΔInc.	ΔFamily Size	ΔSupers	ΔSmalls	Black Prop.	R^2	F
Linear	59-64	-.056	.080 (.072)	.223 (.304)	.198 (.246)	-.452[a] (.139)	-.029 (.030)	.22[a]	3.77[a]
	64-67	-.056	.026[b] (.014)	.043 (.056)	-.542[b] (.314)	-.851[a] (.086)	.075[a] (.016)	.64[a]	23.70[a]
	67-69	-.020	-.003 (.014)	.006 (.046)	-.881[a] (.215)	-.230[a] (.086)	-.012 (.011)	.27[a]	5.12[a]
	69-71	-.022	.015[c] (.011)	.052[b] (.034)	-.357[b] (.211)	-.480[a] (.064)	-.014[b] (.008)	.50[a]	13.76[a]

[a] .01 significance level.
[b] .05 significance level.
[c] .10 significance level.

stores in the ten predominantly black communities where much of the rioting occurred shrank from 539 to 315. Meanwhile, the number of small stores in the six other primarily black areas changed only from 115 to 103.

The most recent period studied, 1969-71, does indicate a relative decrease in small stores and superettes in the inner city communities. This finding may well represent relatively lower profits (or lower expected profits) in inner city stores. For example, the disturbances of 1968 likely resulted in much higher security costs for ghetto merchants.

Chain supermarkets claim to price their products similarly in all areas of a city and price comparison studies have generally confirmed this statement. However, their decisions to locate stores must depend on the profits they can expect and so changes in supermarkets were also of interest in this study. Overall, the supermarket models (Table 6-12) were statistically weak—likely due on the one hand to the relatively greater staying power of supermarkets (due to chain affiliations, size, and so on) and on the other, to their higher start-up costs as compared to small stores or superettes. Still one interesting and disturbing finding emerges—namely that in 1969-71 the number of supermarkets in black areas was decreasing relative to white areas. This result is disturbing because at present supermarkets are the one store class where inner city shoppers can purchase food at prices comparable to those paid in the outer city areas and in the suburbs. If their numbers are relatively decreasing, the plight of ghetto consumers is worsening.

All the above observations can be placed in somewhat clearer perspective by Table 6-13 which shows the number of stores of various types (per estimated food expenditure) in outer and inner city areas. These figures were developed by first classifying the community areas as Outer, Mixed, or Inner City communities depending on the proportion of blacks in each area as of 1960 (same definitions as in preceding chapters). Store numbers were aggregated for each of these three classes of communities and divided by the estimated food expenditures for each class. The appropriate denominator was felt to be estimated food expenditures since it incorporates the effects of both income and family size on demand for food.

Table 6-13 affirms the regression results, namely increases in small stores and superettes in inner city areas relative to outer city areas in 1964-67 and decreases in 1967-69 and 1969-71. In addition, it

Table 6-12
Regression Results: Changes in Supermarkets per Family, 1959-71 (Standard Errors in Parentheses)

Model	Time Interval	Const.	ΔInc.	ΔFamily Size	ΔSupers	ΔSmalls	Black Prop.	R^2	F
Linear	59-64	-.002	.008 (.036)	.039 (.150)	.048 (.059)	-.086 (.073)	-.024[b] (.014)	-.10	1.50
	64-67	-.005	.001 (.005)	.021 (.021)	-.077[b] (.045)	-.062 (.050)	.008 (.007)	.06	.84
	67-69	-.013	.002 (.007)	-.009 (.023)	-.225[a] (.055)	-.059 (.045)	-.003 (.005)	.21[b]	3.51[b]
	69-71	-.001	.004 (.006)	.014 (.019)	-.113[b] (.067)	-.065[c] (.048)	-.011[a] (.004)	.11	1.61

[a] .01 significance level.
[b] .05 significance level.
[c] .10 significance level.

Table 6-13

Percentage Changes in Number of Stores (by Type) per Estimated Food Expenditure, 1959-71

Store Type	Community Type	59-64	64-67	67-69	69-71
Small	Outer City	43	−6	−12	−10
	Mixed City	38	−19	−22	−18
	Inner City	36	9	−34	0
Superette	Outer City	−50	−36	−9	−24
	Mixed City	−53	−11	−8	−20
	Inner City	−48	−9	−5	−42
Supermarket	Outer City	−17	1	−19	7
	Mixed City	−10	−9	−25	−11
	Inner City	−43	4	−13	−21
Weighted Sum	Outer City	−22	−6	−17	−2
	Mixed City	−49	−7	−14	−16
	Inner City	−31	3	−19	−18

discloses some differences in the retail food market in inner and outer city areas. Inner city areas have a larger number of small stores and superettes per estimated food expenditure (or per family).

Weighted Sum of Stores

One might expect that small stores, superettes, and supermarkets in the inner city areas would be of different sizes than such stores in the outer city areas. Data were available to examine this question: 1963 food sales for sixty-nine of the community areas (3).

A regression of food sales versus number of small stores, superettes, and supermarkets should yield estimates of the average size (in dollar sales) of each type of store. Such regressions (with zero-intercept stipulated) were run separately for all Outer City and all Inner City community areas (Table 6-14). Supermarkets in the Outer City areas appeared larger than supermarkets in Inner City areas, a finding consonant with other studies. Inner City area small stores, however, seemed to be relatively large, implying a greater reliance on them by inner city area shoppers than by outer city shoppers.

These last findings enable one to consider the total changes in food retailing in inner city areas relative to outer city areas. For each year, stores of various types in each area were weighted by the

Table 6-14
Regression Results: Food Sales versus Numbers of Stores[a]

Communities	n	Small	Superette	Supermarket	R^2
Outer City	47	36.33 (15.70)	147.17 (52.76)	1139.59 (99.70)	.95
Inner City	14	94.39 (31.25)	109.40 (66.77)	700.66 (115.00)	.98

[a]Standard errors in parentheses.

coefficients in Table 6-14. The results displayed in Table 6-13 confirm earlier observations, especially those regarding the relative drop in grocery stores in black areas between 1969 and 1971.

Finally, one might ask, would weighting stores by their estimated size alter the regression results in Tables 6-10, 6-11, and 6-12. The answer is no. Such regressions were run and produced similar results and are available upon request.

Summary

Data on the operating costs of food stores suggest that costs in the city are higher than those in the suburbs. Within the city, inner city stores incur larger costs than outer city stores. Finally, independent grocery stores are likely to experience greater expenses (as a percentage of sales) than chain stores.

Gross margins of inner city stores, however, are likely to be larger than those enjoyed by outer city stores because of the composition of their food sales. Inner city stores sell relatively more high mark-up meat items (especially pork) than outer city stores and this more than offsets the relatively lower sales of high mark-up grocery items (such as frozen foods) in the inner city.

During the decade of the 60s in Chicago, during certain time intervals, superettes and small food stores were increasing in inner city areas relative to other areas. However, during the most recent period studied (1969-71), small stores, superettes, and super-markets—all were decreasing in the inner city relative to the other parts of the city. That suggests that during the late 60s ghetto area grocers in Chicago were not making the relatively high profits that one would expect were they enjoying any monopoly power.

7

Determining the Optimal Retail Structure for Inner City Areas

Previous chapters presented findings indicating that while average food prices in chain stores were about the same in the suburb, outer city, and inner city areas of Chicago; average food prices in small independent stores were highest in the inner city. When these findings are coupled with the findings that chain stores are relatively less dense in inner city areas and that some inner city shoppers are less mobile and less likely to shop around, the reason that urban poor claim they pay more for food is clear. Generally the shopping choice for a poor family is between a high-price, nearby small store or a lower-price, faraway chain supermarket, the trip to which includes time and transportation cost. Either way they pay more for food.

As Sturdivant observed,

the retail communities in most ghettos are characterized by an atomistic structure with numerous small, owner-operated establishments serving the poor. Such firms lack the managerial sophistication, capital, and capacity to service their market effectively. (39)

And, as discussed in Chapter 6, the apparent relative lack of profits in inner city areas is further weakening the retail structures there.

Yet it may be rash to adopt public policy that would seek to eliminate the small stores even if chain stores might be enticed to replace them. The small or Mom 'n Pop stores may provide the low-income market with unique services such as credit, check cashing, convenient location, convenient hours, and the assembly of items on a shopping list for young children purchasing food for the family. Removal of all small stores and their services might cause hardships for many inner city consumers.

If the problems of poor and black consumers are to be solved, the type of retail structure necessary in the inner city marketplace must be clearly understood so that public policy can be designed to effect the needed changes. This chapter outlines two analytical approaches—graph theory and simulation—that can be used to evaluate existing inner city retail structures and to discover that structure which is optimal for consumers. Although the illustrations for this chapter concern Chicago, both approaches were developed in connection with possible applications for two areas in New York City, one in Harlem and one on the Lower East Side.

Analyzing Retail Structures

Most previous studies of retail structure have not directly approached the question, "What is the best mix of stores by type, number, size, and location?" For example, one recent study was interested only in detecting structural differences among areas (207) not in determining the optimal structure nor even in finding explanations for the existing ones. The studies most related to discovering the retail structure most appropriate to an area have been those concerned with finding the total square footage of a certain store type (for instance, food, clothing) necessary to satisfy the demand of consumers in a given area (140,206). While solving an important problem, such approaches have, however, usually assumed away the more complex problems of deciding how that total square footage should be divided among stores and how those stores should be distributed throughout a community. As Bloom observed,

There is an obvious need for a careful study of the nature of the ghetto environment and for innovative efforts to design a commercial distribution system specifically adapted to the needs and characteristics of the [ghetto] resident. (24)

Questions of retail structure are crucial because their answers in large part determine the quality of retail services the community residents receive. For example, consider the food store services that might be available in an area. At one extreme, a single, extraordinarily large grocery store might be located in the center of a community. In exchange for lower prices (reflecting store-operating economies of scale) and assortment width, the consumers would trade away such benefits as convenience of location, personalized services, and, perhaps, credit availability. The other extreme would consist of numerous small stores—one on every corner—with the same total square footage as the large store. Then trades would be made in the opposite direction. The major contribution of this chapter is to develop a methodology that can be used to examine these trade-offs and so provide insight into the type, size, and location mix of stores that is best suited to the consumers of a given area.

Overall Size of Retail Structure

Before discussing ways to examine the mix of stores in an area (sizes, locations, and so on), it is useful to briefly consider whether one can make any overall observations concerning those areas of a city that may have relatively few or many grocery stores.

Estimates of family food expenditures were made for each of Chicago's seventy-five community areas. Estimated 1960 food expenditures were derived from the median family income and average family size for each community (140). The 1960 figures were projected three years so that they could be compared to community food sales data available for 1963 (3). A community where food expenditures exceed sales might be termed an importer of food; a community where sales are larger than expenditures might be called a food-exporting community.

Table 7-1 corroborates the findings of Chapter 5. As a group, residents of inner city communities were estimated to purchase 12 percent of their food needs outside their communities. It appears likely that those purchases were made mainly in the Mixed City communities (10 percent to 75 percent non-white) since their food sales exceeded estimated food needs by 6 percent. (In Outer City communities, food sales and estimated family expenditures were equal.) These aggregate data do not prove that hypothesis, of course, due to the possibility of compensating shopping trips among black, mixed, and white communities. An independent study did report, though, that 24 percent of respondents from Chicago's South Side claimed that they shopped outside of their area for food (140) and that result would be consistent with the hypothesis that, overall, black communities are food-importing areas.

These findings were consistent for the individual communities within each group. For eight of ten Inner City communities, food expenditures were greater than food sales, but in only 4 of 12 Mixed City communities and 21 of 47 Outer City communities did food expenditures exceed sales.

Table 7-1
Estimated Food Expenditures/Food Sales, by Community, 1963

Community	Number	Retail Food Ratio[a] (1963)
Outer City		
Rogers Park	1	.96
West Ridge	2	1.02
Uptown	3	.90
Lincoln Square	4	1.05
North Center	5	1.18
Lake View	6	.97
Lincoln Park	7	.93
Edison Park	9	n.a.[b]
Norwood Park	10	.89
Jefferson Park	11	1.53
Forest Glen	12	1.50
North Park	13	.78
Albany Park	14	1.62
Portage Park	15	.74
Irving Park	16	.71
Dunning	17	5.05
Montclare	18	.31
Belmont Cragin	19	.79
Hermosa	20	1.12
Avondale	21	1.42
Logan Square	22	1.06
Hamboldt Park	23	1.14
West Town	24	1.36
Austin	25	.86
South Lawndale	30	1.17
Lower West Side	31	1.70
Avalon Park	45	n.a.[b]
South Chicago	46	.77
Burnside	47	n.a.[b]
Calumet Heights	48	1.41
Pullman	50	4.60
South Deering	51	.68
East Side	52	1.18
West Pullman	53	.84
Hegewisch	55	1.60
Garfield Ridge	56	.72
Archer Heights	57	.59
Brighton Park	58	.90
McKinley Park	59	1.04
Bridgeport	60	1.08
New City	61	.72
West Elsdon	62	.87
Gage Park	63	.89
Cleaving	64	.94
West Lawn	65	.80
Chicago Lawn	66	.81
Ashburn	70	.70
Auburn Gresham	71	.82
Beverly	72	1.37
Mount Greenwood	74	.62

Table 7-1 continued

Community	Number	Retail Food Ratio[a] (1963)
Mixed City		
Near North Side	8	1.16
West Garfield Park	26	1.34
East Garfield Park	27	.71
Near West Side	28	.85
The Loop	32	n.a.[b]
Amour Square	34	n.a.[b]
Hyde Park	41	1.05
South Shore	43	1.25
Chatham	44	.76
Roseland	49	.84
West Englewood	67	.87
Englewood	68	.95
Washington Heights	73	.75
Morgan Park	75	.83
Inner City		
North Lawndale	29	1.17
Near South Side	33	1.73
Douglas	35	.99
Oakland	36	1.65
Fuller Park	37	2.21
Grand Boulevard	38	.82
Kenwood	39	1.13
Washington Park	40	1.08
Woodlawn	42	1.21
Riverdale	54	n.a.[b]
Greater Grand Crossing	69	1.07

[a] Food ratio is estimated 1963 food expenditures/1963 food sales.

[b] n.a. means not available.

In sum, that Inner City areas require changes in their current grocery store mix is indicated by the fact that the existing structures in those areas are not serving the needs of the residents.

Graph Theory Approach

Graph theory is concerned with analyzing relations in systems such as electric circuits, transportation networks, or organizations. [See (24) for a helpful survey.] For example, Figure 7-1 might represent wiring in a house, bus routes in New York City, or the relationships among people in a research department. Such a figure is known as a *graph* and consists of *nodes* and *edges*.

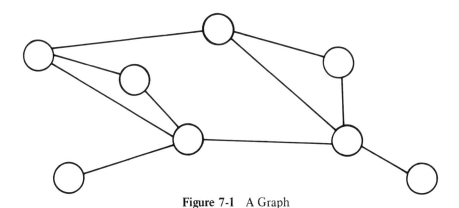

Figure 7-1 A Graph

If one is concerned with the relationship between consumers and grocery stores, then the nodes correspond to families and to food stores. If a particular family shops at a given store, a line connects that family to that store. In Figure 7-2, family 1 shops at stores 1 and 2, but not at store 3.

Graph theory is relevant to the the inner city retail structure problem in at least two ways: (1) evaluating the retail structure in an area, and (2) designing an optimal retail structure for a given area.

Evaluating a Retail Structure

A graph such as that shown in Figure 7-2 reveals the pattern of shopping visits made by a given family to the grocery stores in an area. Such information offers two kinds of insight into a retail structure. First, shopping patterns indicate the existence and size of trading areas—systems of stores and families that are self-contained. Second, by analyzing the store contacts for each individual family,

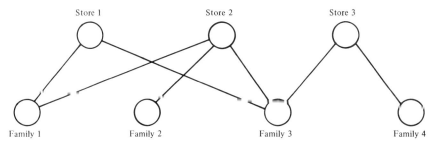

Figure 7-2 Store-Family Graph

one can determine whether or not store preferences are homogeneous across various demographic groups such as low-income families, black families, or families with household heads older than sixty-five. Such information would allow one to more precisely evaluate the impact of removing a certain store or stores from a retail system in a given geographical area.

A specific application of this point concerns the position of small stores in a retail system. If small independent stores provide indispensible services to the urban poor, one would expect that low-income inner city families tend to patronize Mom 'n Pop stores exclusively. On the other hand, if low-income famiies (or subsets of low-income families such as the aged poor) do not require such services of small stores as convenience and credit on each of their shopping trips, then one would expect to observe these families shopping at stores other than small stores.

Most previous studies of contacts between families and stores either have been based on incomplete data or have analyzed data on the aggregate level rather than on an individual family basis. The data of these other studies have been incomplete in the sense that they have not included all the actual contacts between a family and the grocery stores in an area. Instead these researchers have relied on questionnaires to secure the names of the one, two, or three stores at which a housewife claims she usually shops. Other studies, based on more complete data, have analyzed store purchasing patterns by, for example, calculating the proportions of all visits made by families in certain demographic class to small stores or to chain stores. Such aggregation does not allow one to accurately estimate trading areas.

The graph theoretical concept that allows one to analyze family-store contacts on a micro-(individual family) level is that of connectedness. A graph is said to be *connected* if there exists a path connecting any two nodes in the graph (214). The graph in Figure 7-3A is connected; that in Figure 7-3B is disconnected.

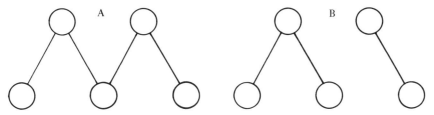

Figure 7-3 Illustrations of Connected (*A*) and Disconnected (*B*) Graphs

It can be shown [see (212)] that for a graph of the sort considered here (no lines permitted between store-nodes or between family-nodes) that:

Number of lines in graph	Description
Fewer than $n - 1$	disconnected
More than $(n_1 - 1)(n_2 - 1) + 1$	connected

Where:

$$n = n_1 + n_2$$

n_1 = Number of stores.

n_2 = Number of families.

If the graph representing all the families and stores in a given area is disconnected, that signifies the presence of two or more separate trading areas in that area. (Notice that "trading area" is being defined in a precise way, namely in terms of family-store contacts. There may be two such trading areas in the same geographic area if some families patronize one set of stores and other families another set of stores.) If one finds such trading areas exist, one next would seek to determine the particular families and stores comprising each. For illustration, low-income, older families and certain small ethnic-oriented stores might form a trading area.

In practice, one would observe only a sample of families in a particular area during a given time interval. Therefore it would be necessary to test the following null hypothesis:

The family-store contacts in area A from a connected graph.

A sample statistic that can be used to test that hypothesis is:

I = Connectedness index.

$$= \frac{e - (n_1 + n_2 - 2)}{[((n_1 - 1)(n_2 - 1) + 2) - (n_1 + n_2 - 2)]}$$

$$\text{for } n_1 + n_2 - 1 \leqslant e \leqslant (n_1 - 1)(n_2 - 1) + 1$$

$$= 0 \text{ for } e < n_1 + n_2 - 1$$

$$= 1 \text{ for } e > (n_1 - 1)(n_2 - 1) + 1$$

Where:

e = number of edges (store-family contacts) in graph;

n_1 = number of families in sample; and

n_2 = number of stores in area corresponding to sample families

The sampling distribution for I can be derived, although it is mathematically cumbersome to do so [see 212)]. Generally however, the larger the value of I, the more likely that the graph of that retail system will be connected.

An illustrative application of graph theory to detect shopping patterns was made based on panel data from the Family Survey Bureau of the Chicago *Tribune.* The data consist of all the purchases of coffee, instant coffee, and tea made by 600 families over a two-and-one-half year period beginning in the fall of 1963. These data were described in detail in Chapter 3. Their main advantage for this investigation is their completeness: all contacts between families and stores (excepting reporting errors) were available.

For illustration, twelve of the seventy-five community areas in Chicago were examined. These included areas with relatively few blacks, with similar proportions of blacks and whites, and with relatively few whites. For each area the number of stores, n_1, the number of sampled families, n_2, and the number of reported contacts between families and stores, e, were used to calculate a value for I.

Table 7-2 displays the results. Notice that the retail structures used by whites tend more toward connectedness (6 of 7 I-values above .35) than those corresponding to blacks (only 4 of 10 above .35). These findings are consistent with more shopping mobility for the white families. Were this analysis not simply an example of methodology, it would likely be useful to pursue this result by grouping families by income as well as race.

Designing an Optimal Retail Structure

Determining the optimal structure for a retail system can be viewed as a network problem. A network is a particular kind of graph, namely a graph with flows of some type through its edges. For example, the street system of a city is a network—the nodes are

Table 7-2
Connectedness in Food Retail Systems: Illustrative Findings for Selected Community Areas in Chicago

Area	Blacks as % of Population (1960)	Whites Alone	Value of I Blacks Alone	All
22	.8	.42		.42
23	.9	.71	1.	.29
24	2.3	.36	.45	.17
25	.1	.18	.22	.18
43	10.4	.38	.38	.29
41	40.3	1.	*	.33
27	62.0		.24	.24
28	54.4	1.	.20	.17
68	69.2		.18	.18
38	99.5		.18	.18
40	99.2		.0	.0
42	89.6		.40	.40

*Only one family—I cannot be meaningfully computed.

intersections, the edges are the streets, and the flow consists of traffic.

In the graph, theoretic representation of the inner city food retailing system, the nodes were defined as stores and families and the edges as visits by a family to a store. That model is made more realistic by defining the flows between the nodes. The most straightforward approach is to define these flows to be the amounts of various food goods moving from store to customer. That is:

x_{ij} = amount of specific food purchased by family i in store j.

Each store can be described by a set of attributes such as geographical distance from a family, the hours that the store is open, credit, service, and so forth. Define the "length" of an edge to be:

$$d_{ij} = \left[\sum_k w_k (a_k - a_k^*)^2 \right]^{1/2}$$

Where:

a_k = family i's evaluation of store j on attribute k;

a_k^* = family i's ideal value for attribute k; and

w_k = importance of attribute k to family i.

Given those definitions, network theory can be used to solve the following two sorts of problems:

1. Determine the properties (number of stores, sizes of stores, and locations) of a retail structure that will serve all families in a given area. This problem is basically a variation of the well-known "minimal spanning tree problem."

2. Predict the effects of modifying a current retail structure by deleting, moving, or adding stores. To solve this problem, one would employ, on an individual family level, the type of flow analysis used by White and Ellis (216).

It would not be appropriate to discuss the mathematical theory in this book. The interested reader can find a lucid explanation in *Introduction to Operations Research* (208).

Simulation Approach

A simulation is a computerized model of some system (211). Rules and numbers are given to the computer so it can behave as if it were, say, a network of streets or an assembly line. By changing the rules and numbers, one can infer what would happen in the real world were similar changes made. For example, with a simulation of the streets in Manhattan, one could determine the effects on traffic flow if the timing of street lights were changed or if certain streets were made one-way.

Informally, one might term simulations "What if. . . ." models. They function as laboratories for situations that would be difficult to experiment with in real life. One can easily imagine, for example, the resulting confusion if on a day-to-day basis one changed the timing of streetlights or the direction of traffic flow in streets.

Typically, simulations are used for problems dealing with systems where there are many complex relations and where events happen with uncertainty. A marketplace is such a system. The relationships linking people to stores are complicated and not generally well-understood. The times they go shopping and the products, brands, and package sizes they buy vary stochastically.

To consider alternate mixes of stores, a simulation of retail shopping behavior was constructed. (The FORTRAN program is available on request.) As shown in the flow chart in Figure 7-4, customer entrances to the simulated marketplace are randomly generated. The race and income class of each customer, as well as his address, are randomly determined as he enters the system, according to the demographic make-up of the community.

Of the three or four food shopping trips people make each week, some are major trips, others are fill-in trips when only a few items are purchased. For each simulated customer, the number of items he plans to purchase, a function of his race and income class and the particular time period being simulated, is randomly determined. In turn, whether the trip is major or minor affects the type store (supermarket or small store) the customer may consider visiting. If it is a major trip, he is likely to shop at a supermarket to the extent he is relatively mobile. A minor shopping trip may be made either to a supermarket or to a smaller store.

The simulated customer sets out for the closest store of the type (or types) consonant with the nature of his shopping trip. Depending on the distance to the store, he or she will either walk, drive, or take public transportation. The products purchased are randomly determined according to his or her past behavior.

Recorded for each simulated trip are the time and money required to reach the store and the time and money spent in the store. These amounts, when summarized, are broken down by race and income class.

Trial Applications

For illustration, the simulation was applied to (1) a generalized area and (2) the Hyde Park section of Chicago as it was in 1967. The generalized area allowed comparisons of idealized retail structures such as uniform distributions of supermarkets or small stores. Hyde Park (selected for both the heterogeneity of its population and the author's first-hand knowledge of its shopping patterns) served as a limited example of how the simulation might be used to suggest changes in an existing retail structure.

Estimates for some of the parameters of the simulation were obtained from several sources (3, 20). Such data included the number and type of stores (supermarket, superette, small store) in each area and the relative prices among store types, as well as the

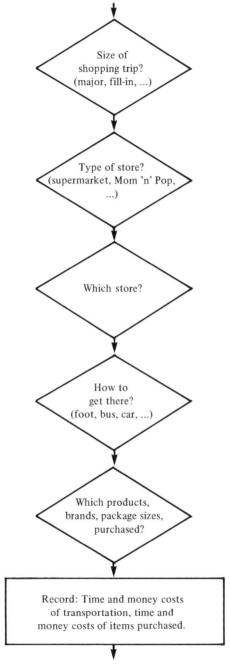

Figure 7-4 Simulated Shopping Trip

race and income distributions of residents of Chicago communities and the sizes and frequencies of shopping trips made by consumers of various demographic groups.

In both illustrations, consumers in the low-income class were considered to make more frequent shopping trips for fewer items than those in the other income classes. Due to their relative lack of mobility, low-income shoppers were, for these illustrations, assumed to always shop at the nearest of all stores, while consumers of higher income classes would shop only at the nearest supermarket when making a major shopping trip.

Generalized Area

The area was arbitrarily assumed to be one mile square and the population equally divided among blacks and whites. Consumers of each race and income group were all assumed to be uniformly distributed throughout the area.

Four different retail structures were selected as preliminary examples (Figure 7-5). One thousand simulated shopping trips were made through each, and the means and standard deviations of the time and money spent traveling to the store and the time and money spent in the store recorded. Only a few of these statistics are shown in Table 7-3 since for these few simple examples the results were not

Table 7-3
Results for Generalized Area

| | | Race and Income | | | | | |
| | | White | | | Black | | |
	Structure	Low	Middle	High	Low	Middle	High
Price per item	1	1.00	1.00	1.00	1.00	1.00	1.00
	2	1.00	1.00	1.00	1.00	1.00	1.00
	3	1.05	1.05	1.05	1.05	1.05	1.00
	4	1.05	1.01	1.01	1.06	1.00	1.00
Distance per	1	5.0	5.2	5.0	5.1	5.2	5.2
trip	2	2.2	2.3	2.3	2.2	2.2	2.1
	3	1.0	1.0	1.0	1.0	1.0	1.0
	4	1.7	2.4	2.4	1.6	2.3	2.3
Supermarket trips	1	1.00	1.00	1.00	1.00	1.00	1.00
as proportion of	2	1.00	1.00	1.00	1.00	1.00	1.00
all trips	3	.00	.00	.00	.00	.00	.00
	4	.41	.93	.92	.33	.95	.94

startling: low-income families paid more under the mixed (and most realistic) retail structure, structure 4.

The main point of the findings in Table 7-3 is to show how simulation can provide insights on several dimensions important to the consumer. Price and distance (which can be translated into time and money costs) is a major trade-off to be considered in designing a retail structure. Other dimensions, such as product assortment and services available, can also be built into the model and reported. In evaluating such results, one must keep in mind that certain aspects of

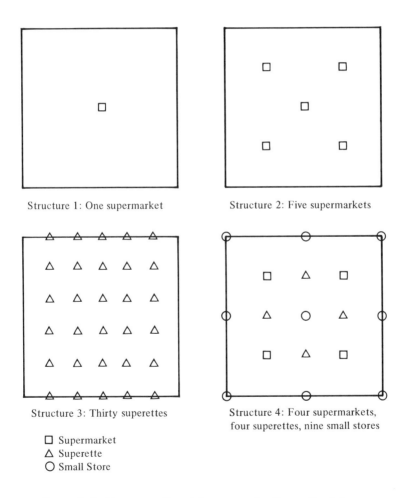

Structure 1: One supermarket

Structure 2: Five supermarkets

Structure 3: Thirty superettes

Structure 4: Four supermarkets, four superettes, nine small stores

□ Supermarket
△ Superette
○ Small Store

Figure 7-5 Alternative Retail Structures for Generalized Area

the structure may be more important to certain demographic groups than to others.

Hyde Park

Hyde Park comprises roughly one square mile. In 1967, 59 percent of its population was white. Although it is a well-integrated community, there are some residence patterns related to race and income, and these were included in the model's parameters.

The 1967 retail structure and four others were examined (Figure 7-6), structures 4 and 5 being possible alternatives to the existing structure. As shown in Table 7-4, the structure omitting the small stores and repositioning one supermarket and some of the superettes, structure 5, resulted in lower prices and distances for all consumer classes. Although the movement of the small stores and superettes would likely not be feasible, the addition of another supermarket on the West section of 55th Street might usefully be considered if this were a real application. In fact, a supermarket was located there in 1966, but was urban-renewed out of existence. Other sites and other structures, of course, might be evaluated with the simulation.

Table 7-4
Results for Hyde Park (1967)

| | | Race and Income | | | | | |
| | | White | | | Black | | |
	Structure	Low	Middle	High	Low	Middle	High
Price per item	1	1.07	1.00	1.01	1.05	1.01	1.01
	2	1.00	1.00	1.00	1.00	1.00	1.00
	3	1.07	1.07	1.07	1.07	1.06	1.06
	4	1.07	1.01	1.01	1.06	1.01	1.01
	5	1.04	1.00	1.00	1.04	1.00	1.01
Distance per	1	2.2	2.9	4.5	1.6	3.0	2.8
trip	2	4.1	3.2	5.3	3.0	3.5	3.7
	3	2.1	1.9	2.1	1.7	1.9	1.6
	4	2.1	3.3	4.7	1.7	3.2	3.2
	5	1.7	2.5	3.1	1.4	2.4	2.5
Supermarket trips	1	.14	.93	.92	.20	.93	.91
as proportion of	2	1.00	1.00	1.00	1.00	1.00	1.00
all trips	3	.00	.00	.00	.00	.00	.00
	4	.10	.91	.90	.11	.92	.84
	5	.21	.93	.91	.15	.92	.87

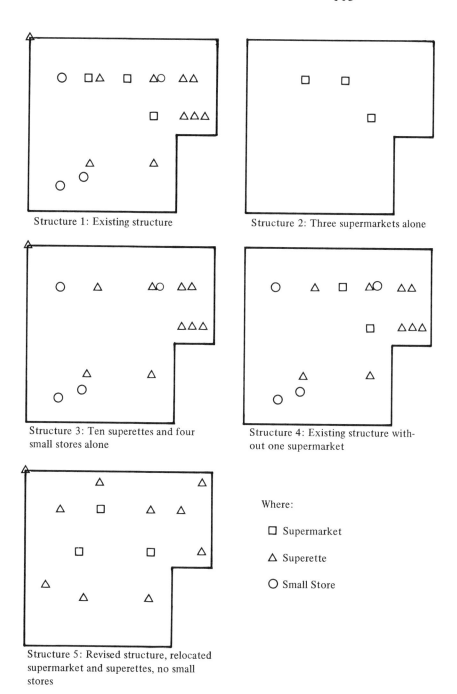

Structure 1: Existing structure

Structure 2: Three supermarkets alone

Structure 3: Ten superettes and four small stores alone

Structure 4: Existing structure without one supermarket

Structure 5: Revised structure, relocated supermarket and superettes, no small stores

Where:

□ Supermarket

△ Superette

○ Small Store

Figure 7-6 Alternative Retail Structures for Hyde Park (1967)

Possible Extensions to the Simulation

There are obvious ways in which this particular simulation model might be improved. First, customers might be more thoroughly described—by age, family size, and automobile ownership—and their purchase habits more completely detailed. Second, the selection of store type and the particular store shopped would be made more realistic by explicitly including other store characteristics such as perceived service, prices, and product quality, and by considering mixed shopping trips, for instance, food and clothing, and one-way shopping trips, such as purchases made on the return from work. Third, transportation choices might be more varied, including going to the store on foot and returning by taxi.

Summary

The problem of evaluating a retail structure is multi-faceted. Static approaches to the problem miss the details that determine the quality of retail services. Examining retail services from only a square footage basis ignores the various criteria consumers employ to rate stores. Graph theory and Monte Carlo simulation are two approaches that can simultaneously incorporate many factors and markedly improve analysis of retail structures.

8   Overview

Chapter 1 began with quotations from five persons very much involved with groceries in the ghetto marketplace: two were heads of consumer action groups in Washington and in New York, two represented chain-store management, the other was an independent grocer in Detroit's inner city. At first glance their statements appeared at odds with each other. Now, in the light of the discussions in Chapters 2 through 7, it should be clear that all their observations were correct given their own particular viewpoints.

Methodology

The charts and graphs that we have prepared ... point up without question the unfair [food] pricing practices which exist [in the inner city] .... (99)

This observation was made by a participant in a study that suffered from such methodological problems as small sample size and likely misclassification of stores. It illustrates the point that price comparison studies require more rigorous research designs and executions than most laymen realize. In particular, selection of time periods, stores, products, brands, and package sizes must be precisely specified. If not, no matter how well-meaning or how much effort is placed in such studies, their conclusions must remain suspect.

Price Differences

There is no truth in the accusation that Safeway charges higher prices .... (99)

These prices are the same in the approximately 450 A & P stores in that area. (99)

Overall prices in stores of the same chain were found to be similar

115

among suburb, outer city, and inner city areas. These results were obtained with two quite different data bases for the Chicago Metropolitan Area during the decade of the 60s. There *were* price differences in chain stores for specific products, but these differences did not form any continuing systematic pattern. That is, there were items in inner city stores that were priced both higher *and* lower than in chain stores elsewhere.

Independent store prices did show a distinct pattern. On the whole prices were highest in the inner city and lowest in the suburbs for such product groups as beverages, packaged goods, and laundry and cleaning products.

Shopping Patterns

In our Bedford-Stuyvesant community, the residents have been asking themselves on a day-to-day basis, why is it that they pay such high prices, particularly for food? (99)

The answer to that question begins with the structure of food retailing typically found in the inner city: Mom 'n Pop stores are relatively plentiful, and chain supermarkets are relatively sparse. In fact, if one maps the locations of chain stores in Chicago in 1969, those in the inner city area are generally found on its borders with other sections of the city (93).

Inner city shoppers generally appear to fall into one of two groups: Those who are relatively mobile (perhaps because they own cars) and who travel to chain stores outside their neighborhoods, and those who are relatively immobile (perhaps because they lack cars and have young children) and who shop at small independent stores that are close-by.

Those who shop at the Mom 'n Pop stores are clearly paying more for food. Those who go to chain stores may also be paying more if their travel costs exceed those of shoppers in the outer city or suburban areas.

Operating Costs, Margins, and Profits

Sure I have to charge more than a chain store in the suburbs, but my overhead, risks, and losses are a helluva lot more than anybody's in the suburbs. Even with my higher prices, I make less profit than they do. (62)

The available evidence regarding operating costs is shaky, but what reliable data there are indicate grocery store operating costs are higher in the inner city, especially for independent stores. Payroll appears to account for much of this difference.

It is likely that gross margins are somewhat higher for inner city supermarkets, even among stores charging identical prices for similar items. The reason is the difference in the mixes of products sold by inner city supermarkets and by stores elsewhere. "Soul" meats have higher mark-ups than other meat items, therefore making the gross margin for the meat operation of an inner city food store relatively high. In fact, the relatively high meat gross margin is sufficiently large to offset the relatively low gross margins for groceries and produce sold in the inner city.

A corollary to the above observation is that small independent stores without appreciable meat sales cannot tolerate relatively low margins on grocery and produce. They must earn their profits on grocery and produce items.

Operating costs and gross margins together determine profits. Rather than attempting to relate operating cost and margin data from widely differing sources, this study examined profitability by looking at the results of profits: If profits are exorbitantly high in an area and there are no barriers to entry, then the number of stores should increase relative to other areas. If profits are relatively low, other things being equal, the relative number of stores should fall.

During the mid-60s, small stores and superettes were increasing in Chicago's inner city relative to the outer city. (More precisely, they were decreasing less rapidly.) However, in the late-60s, the numbers of small stores and superettes (and supermarkets too) in Chicago's inner city were decreasing relative to the outer city—a result consistent with relatively *lower* profits in the inner city.

Price Discrimination

The poor do pay more! Let's get that out of the way right at the beginning. In the inner city, the poor are dealing with a handful of independents who expect trouble every second, who pay exorbitant rates for insurance, when they can afford it, and who charge accordingly. Their overhead determines their prices. They're not price gougers. (73)

In economic theory, price discrimination is said to occur when different persons are charged different prices for identical items. When examining grocery products, one must keep in mind that even the same brand and package size of, say, cereal may, when sold in different stores, be differentiated by the different mix of services each store offers.

If at the checkout counters of a given store at a specific time, two persons were each charged a different price for a 12-ounce package of brand X cereal, that would be a clear case of price discrimination. Most allegations of grocery price discrimination do not suggest that discrimination is taking place in such fashion. Rather, the type of food price discrimination usually alleged is de facto discrimination, where shoppers in certain areas pay more for the same item than shoppers elsewhere. However, when one is comparing products purchased in different stores, in order to substantiate allegations of price discrimination one must somehow allow for service differences among stores.

While services offered by stores of the same chain may differ to some degree, one may expect them to be more similar than the services extended by stores of various chains. Stores of the same chain were generally found to charge similar prices for the same product. To the extent that services among stores of a given chain are the same, this study found no evidence of price discrimination practiced by chains against inner city shoppers.

Whether there is de facto price discrimination among independent stores is much more difficult to ascertain. Their services likely differ considerably among suburban, outer city, and inner city areas as well as within areas. Perhaps the most effective way to analyze the situation is to operationally equate de facto price discrimination with exorbitant profits, that is, "price gouging." According to the findings of this study, de facto price discrimination against black and low-income shoppers may have existed among Chicago independent stores in the mid-60s, but likely did not exist in the late 60s when inner city small stores and superettes were declining in number relative to other areas.

Solutions

Whether or not an economist would label a situation as "de facto price discrimination" is probably of very, very little import to an inner city shopper buying food for a family. Much more important to that individual are ways to lower food prices or ways to increase the quality of food purchased at a given price.

Alternate strategies for improving inner-city food retailing have been set forth elsewhere (21, 28, 41). They range from starting food cooperatives to offering investment funds to entrepreneurs, to providing tax incentives to chains to locate in the inner city. Whether or not there is one best approach, the author is in doubt. However, one can list some of the issues an effective program must consider:

a. the lack of supermarkets in inner city areas;

b. the relative decrease of all types of food stores in inner city areas;

c. the lack of mobility of many (but not all) black and low-income shoppers;

d. the particular mix of services needed or desired by inner-city area shoppers;

e. the particular mix of products needed or desired by inner-city area families; and

f. the employment of inner-city area residents by food stores.

This book has sought to describe the problem; hopefully it may serve as a basis for the development of the needed solutions.

Bibliography

Primary References

1. *Chain Store Age. 1969 Supermarket Sales Manual.* Chicago: Chain Store Age, 1969.

2. Chicago Community Renewal Program. *An Atlas of Chicago's People, Jobs, and Homes.* Chicago: Chicago Community Renewal Program, 1963.

3. *Chicago Sun-Times/Daily News. Grocery Store Route List, City of Chicago and Suburbs, 1966 Edition.* Chicago: *Chicago Sun-Times/Daily News,* 1966. Also 1968, 1970, and 1972 editions.

4. Earle, Wendell, and John Sheehan. *Operating Results of Food Chains, 1964-65.* Ithaca, N.Y.: Cornell University Press, 1966.

5. Hauser, Philip M., and Evelyn M. Kitagawa, eds. *Local Community Fact Book for Chicago, 1950.* Chicago: Chicago Community Inventory, University of Chicago, 1953.

6. Hodge, Patricia, and Evelyn M. Kitagawa. *Population Projections for the City of Chicago and the Chicago Metropolitan Area, 1970 and 1980.* Chicago: Chicago Community Inventory, University of Chicago, May 1964.

7. Hospital Planning Council for Metropolitan Chicago. *Population Estimates for Municipalities and Counties in the Chicago Consolidated Area: 1965 and 1966.* Chicago: Chicago Association of Commerce and Industry, Dec. 1966.

8. Hospital Planning Council for Metropolitan Chicago. *Population Estimates for Municipalities and Counties in the Chicago Consolidated Area: 1967 and 1968.* Chicago: Chicago Association of Commerce and Industry, July 1968.

9. Kitagawa, Evelyn M., and De Ver Sholes, eds. *Chicagoland's Retail Market.* Chicago: Chicago Association of Commerce and Industry, 1957.

10. ____ , and Karl E. Taeuber, eds. *Local Community Fact Book, Chicago Metropolitan Area, 1960.* Chicago: Chicago Community Inventory, University of Chicago, 1963.

11. *Progressive Grocer. 36th Annual Report of the Grocery Industry.* New York: Progressive Grocer, 1969.

12. De Ver Sholes, ed. *Chicagoland's Retail Market.* Chicago: Chicago Association of Commerce and Industry, 1967.

13. *Supermarket News. Distribution of Food Store Sales in 280 Cities.* New York: Fairchild Publications, 1969.

14. United States Bureau of the Census. *Statistical Abstract of the United States, 1969.* Washington, D. C.: Government Printing Office, 1969. 1967, and 1968 editions also used.

15. United States Department of Agriculture. *Food Consumption of Households in the United States.* Washington, D. C.: Government Printing Office, 1965.

16. United States Department of Commerce. *Business Statistics.* Washington, D. C.: Government Printing Office, Oct. 1971.

17. ____ . "Estimates of the Population of Counties and Metropolitan Areas, July 1, 1966, A Summary Report," *Population Estimates and Projections,* July 31, 1969, p. 71.

18. ____ . "Estimates of the Population of 100 Large Metropolitan Areas: 1967 and 1968," *Population Estimates and Projections,* Oct. 3 1969, p. 3.

19. ____ . "Projections of the Populations of Metropolitan Areas: 1975," *Population Estimates and Projections,* Jan. 31, 1969, p. 69.

20. ____ . *United States Censuses of Population and Housing: 1960, Chicago, Illinois* and *1970, Chicago, Illinois.* Washington, D. C.: Government Printing Office, 1962.

Secondary References

The Ghetto Marketplace

21. Andreasen, Alan R., ed. *Improving Inner City Marketing.* Chicago: American Marketing Association, 1972.

22. Batchelder, Alan. "Poverty: The Special Case of the Negro." *Papers and Proceedings of the Seventy-Ninth Annual Meeting of the American Economic Association.* Chicago, 1964.

23. Becker, Gary S. *The Economics of Discrimination.* Chicago: University of Chicago Press, 1957.

24. Bloom, Gordon F., "Black Capitalism in Ghetto Supermarkets: Problems and Prospects," *Industrial Management Review,* 11 (Spring 1970): 37-48.

25. Brown, James K., and Seymour Lusterman. *Business and the Development of Ghetto Enterprise.* New York: The Conference Board, 1971.

26. Caplovitz, David. "The Merchant and the Low Income Consumer," in *Poverty in America.* L. A. Ferman, et al., eds., Ann Arbor, Mich.: University of Michigan Press, 1965.

27. ____ . *The Poor Pay More.* New York: The Free Press, 1967.

28. Cox, William E., Jr., and Sue R. Seidman, "Cooperatives in the Ghetto," *Proceedings of the 1969 Summer Conference of the American Marketing Association.* Chicago: American Marketing Assoc., 1969.

29. Fogelson, Robert M. "White on Black: A Critique of the McCone Commission Report on the Los Angeles Riots," *Political Science Quarterly* 82 (Sept. 1967): 356ff.

30. Gillen, Ralph L. "A Challenge for Business: Better Commercial Services in Low-Income Neighborhoods." *Proceedings, United States Department of Commerce, Second National Marketing Conference with the National Marketing Advisory Committee.* Washington, D. C.: Government Printing Office, 1968.

31. Jones, Mary Gardner. "The Revolution of Rising Expectations: The Ghetto's Challenge to American Business." Address before the 34th Annual Meeting of the National Association of Food Chains, Nov. 16, 1967.

32. Karpel, Craig. "Ghetto Fraud on the Installment Plan." *New York* 2 (May 26, 1969): 24-32, and 2 (June 2, 1969): 41-4.

33. Levitan, Sar A., and Robert Taggart, III, "Developing Business in the Ghetto," *Conference Board Record,* July 1969, 13-21.

34. Magnuson, W. G., and J. Casper, *The Dark Side of the Marketplace.* Englewood Cliffs, N. J.: Prentice-Hall, 1968.

35. Minichiello, Robert J., "The Real Challenge of Food Discounters," *Journal of Marketing* 31 (April 1967): 37-42.

36. National Advisory Committee on Civil Disorders. *Report of the National Advisory Commission on Civil Disorders.* New York: Bantam Books, 1968.

37. Ornati, Oscar. *Poverty Amid Affluence.* New York: Twentieth Century Fund, 1966.

38. *Progressive Grocer.* "Can Black-Run Supers Fill the Inner-City Void?" *36th Annual Report of the Grocery Industry.* New York: Progressive Grocer, 1969.

39. Sturdivant, Frederick D. "Better Deal for Ghetto Shoppers." *Harvard Business Review* 46 (March-April 1968): 130-9.

40. _____ . *The Ghetto Marketplace.* New York: Free Press, 1969.

41. _____ . "Retailing in the Ghetto: Problems and Proposals." *Proceedings of the 1968 Fall Conference of the American Marketing Association.* Chicago, 1968.

42. *Supermarket News.* "Ralph Sells It Like It Is—Soul Food." July 14, 1969, p. 5.

43. Thompson, Donald L. "Consumer Convenience and Retail Structure," *Journal of Marketing Research* 4 (Feb. 1967): 37-45.

44. United States Congress. Senate. Subcommittee on Employment, Manpower, and Poverty, Committee on Labor and Public Welfare. *Washington Inner City Poverty Survey.* Washington, D. C.: Government Printing Office, Dec. 1968.

45. United States Department of Commerce. *Status Report of Task Force on Commercial Services to Slum Areas.* Washington, D. C.: Government Printing Office, March 20, 1968.

Grocery Store Prices: Studies and Reactions to Studies

46. Adamy, Clarence G. Press release from President, National Association of Food Chains, Washington, D. C., Nov. 6, 1967.

47. *Advertising Age.* "Safeway Denies Charges of Overpricing Foods in Lower Income Neighborhoods." Nov. 23, 1967, p. 34.

48. Alcaly, Roger E. "Food Prices in Relation to Income Levels in New York City," *Journal of Business,* (1972).

49. Alexis, Marcus, and Leonard S. Simon. "The Food Marketing Commission and Food Prices by Income Groups," *Journal of Farm Economics* 49 (May 1967): 439-40.

50. Better Business Bureau of Greater St. Louis. *Comparative Study: Food Prices and Quality Practices of Major Chains in the St. Louis, Missouri Metropolitan Area.* St. Louis, Mo.: Better Business Bureau of Greater St. Louis, 1968.

51. Bjorklund, Einar, and James L. Palmer. *A Study of the Prices of Chain and Independent Grocers in Chicago.* Chicago: University of Chicago Press, 1930.

52. Black, Guy. "Variations in Prices Paid for Food as Affected by Income Level," *Journal of Farm Economics* 34 (Feb. 1952): 52-66.

53. Burk, Marguerite C. "Ramifications of the Relationship Between Income and Food," *Journal of Farm Economics* 44 (Feb. 1962): 105-25.

54. *Chicago Sun Times,* "Survey Shows Food Prices Higher in Hunger Areas," June 2, 1969, p. 11.

55. Conway, Edward B. "A Comparison of Retail Food Prices in Food Chain Outlets—Poverty Area Versus Non-Poverty Area Stores." Unpublished M.S. thesis, St. Louis University, 1967.

56. Dames, Joan F. "Food Prices Found Higher in Slum Areas." St. Louis *Post Dispatch,* Nov. 30, 1967, pp. 1, 15.

57. *Detroit Free Press.* "City Asked to Protect Consumers," Sept. 6, 1968, p. 5-A.

58. ____ . "Detroit Poor Charged More," Sept. 5, 1968, p. 4-B.

59. ____ . "Fear of Whites' Attitudes Ties Blacks to High Prices," Sept. 5, 1968, p. 4-B.

60. ____ . "Self-Help and Study Can Cut Food Costs," Sept. 6, 1968, p. 6-A.

61. ____ . "Shoppers in Inner City Do Pay More and Here's Why." Sept. 5,1968, p. 4-B.

62. *Detroit News.* "And the Grocers Tell Their Side." Sept. 8, 1968, pp. 1H, 12H.

63. ____ . "What Happened When Suburban Women Went Inner City Grocery Shopping." Sept. 8, 1968, p. 1H.

64. Dixon, Donald F., and Daniel J. McLaughlin, Jr. "Do the Inner City Poor Pay More for Food?" *The Economic and Business Bulletin* (School of Business Administration, Temple University, Philadelphia) 20 (Spring 1968): 6-12.

65. ____ . "Do the Poor Really Pay More for Food?" Unpublished paper, Temple University, 1969.

66. Doman, L. "A Study in Price Differences in Retail Grocery

Stores in New York State." *Agricultural Experiment Station Bulletin 665.* Ithaca, N. Y.: Cornell University, 1937.

67. Federal Trade Commission. *Economic Report on Food Chain Selling Practices in the District of Columbia and San Francisco.* Washington, D. C.: Government Printing Office, 1969.

68. Focus: Hope, Inc. *Comparison of Grocery and Drug Prices and Services in the Greater Detroit Area.* Detroit: Catholic Archdiocese of Detroit, 1968.

69. *Food Dealer.* "Is Survey Another Barrage of Industry Criticism?" Aug. 1968, p. 8.

70. Frank, Ronald E., Paul E. Green and H. F. Sieber, Jr. "Household Correlates of Purchase Prices for Grocery Products," *Journal of Marketing Research* 4 (Feb. 1967): 54-8.

71. Goodman, Charles S. "Do the Poor Pay More?" *Journal of Marketing* 32 (Jan. 1968): 18-24.

72. ____ . "Do the Poor Pay More? A Study of the Food Purchasing Practices of Low-Income Consumers." Unpublished paper, University of Pennsylvania, 1967.

73. *Grocers' Spotlight.* "The Poor Do Pay More!" May 6, 1968, p. 3.

74. Groom, Phyllis. "Prices in Poor Neighborhoods." *Illustrated in Monthly Labor Review,* Oct. 1966, pp. 1085-91.

75. Hirsch, Werner Z. "Grocery Chain Store Prices—A Case Study," *Journal of Marketing* 21 (July 1956): 9-23.

76. Human Development Corporation. *Initial Report on the Survey of Food Prices in the St. Louis City and Surrounding Country.* St. Louis, Mo.: Human Development Corporation, Nov. 1, 1967.

77. Lindgren, Donald A. "Pricing Practices of Food Supermarkets in Arizona," *Arizona Business Bulletin* (May 1963): 10-14.

78. Marcus, Burton H. "Similarity of Ghetto and Nonghetto Food Costs," *Journal of Marketing Research* 6 (Aug. 1969): 365-8.

79. *Marketing News* "Poor Pay More? Congressman to D.C. Chapter." Mid-March 1968, p. 1.

80. Millican, Richard D. and Ramone Jean Rogers, "Price Variability of Non-Branded Food Items Among Food Stores in Champaign-Urbana," *Journal of Marketing* 18 (Jan. 1954): 282-4.

81. *Modern Grocer.* "Wright Study," Feb. 19, 1968, pp. 1, 6.

82. Morris, John D. "Merchants Found Deceiving the Poor," *The New York Times,* July 9, 1968, p. 12.

83. National Commission on Food Marketing. "Retail Food Prices in Low and Higher Income Areas: A Study of Prices Charged in Food Stores Located in Low and Higher Income Areas of Six Large Cities, February, 1966." *Special Studies in Food Marketing, Technical Study No. 10.* Washington, D. C.: Government Printing Office, 1966.

84. New Jersey Office of Consumer Protection. *Food Price Comparison Study—August, 1967.* Unpublished report of Newark, N. J., study, Aug. 1967.

85. Phillips, Charles F. "Chain, Voluntary Chain, and Independent Grocery Store Prices, 1930 and 1934," *Journal of Business* 8 (May 1935): 143-9.

86. Rasmussen, M. P., F. A. Quitslund, and E. W. Cake. "Fruit and Vegetable Stores as Retail Outlets for Fruit," *Cornell University Agricultural Experiment Station Bulletin No. 815.* Ithaca, N.Y.: Cornell University, 1940.

87. Ridgeway, James. "Studies in the Grocery Trade," *New Republic,* June 25, 1966, pp. 5-7.

88. Rosenthal, Benjamin S. Press release in Washington, D. C., July 25, 1969.

89. *St. Louis Globe-Democrat.* "Globe Survey of Supermarkets —Poverty Area and Suburb Food Prices Identical," Jan. 18, 1968.

90. ____ . "Globe Survey Reveals Prices at Supermarkets Reflect Competition." Jan. 19, 1968.

91. *St. Louis Post Dispatch.* "Food Prices Rise Linked to Lack of Competition." Jan. 3, 1968.

92. Sexton, Donald E., Jr., "Comparing the Costs of Food to Blacks and to Whites: A Survey," *Journal of Marketing* 35 (July 1971): 40-47; Reprinted in Conrad Berenson, ed., *The Social Dynamics of Marketing.* New York: Random House, 1973.

93. ____ , "Do Blacks Pay More?" *Journal of Marketing Research* 8 (Nov. 1971): 420-6.

94. ____ , "Do Inner City Chains Charge More?" *Journal of Consumer Affairs* (Winter 1973).

95. ____ , "Grocery Prices Paid by Blacks and Whites: Further

Findings," *Journal of Economics and Business* 25 (Fall 1972): 39-44.

96. Task Force on Public Aid of the Church Federation of Greater Chicago. "Summary of Results of Food Pricing Survey." Press release, June 1969.

97. Teach, Richard. *Supermarket Pricing Practices in Various Areas of a Large City.* Buffalo, N. Y.: State University of New York at Buffalo, 1969.

98. U. S. Bureau of Labor Statistics. *Retail Food Prices in Low and Higher Income Areas.* Washington, D. C.: Government Printing Office, 1969.

99. U. S. Congress. House. Subcommittee of the Committee on Government Operations. *Consumer Problems of the Poor: Supermarket Operations in Low-Income Areas and the Federal Response—Hearings.* Washington, D. C.: Government Printing Office, 1968.

100. U. S. Congress. Subcommittee of the Committee on Government Operations. *Consumer Problems of the Poor: Supermarket Operations in Low-Income Areas and the Federal Response—Report.* Washington, D. C.: Government Printing Office, 1968.

101. U. S. Department of Agriculture. *Comparison of Prices Paid for Selected Foods in Chainstores in High and Low Income Areas of Six Cities.* Washington, D. C.: Government Printing Office, 1968.

102. ____ . "Effect of Weekend Prices on U. S. Average Food Prices." *Marketing and Transportation Situation,* Nov. 1968, pp. 3-5.

103. U. S. Department of Agriculture. *Food Prices Before and After Distribution of Welfare Checks.* Washington, D. C.: Government Printing Office, 1970.

104. *Wall Street Journal.* "The Inner City Poor Found to Pay More for Food than Others," Sept. 6, 1968.

105. *Washington Food Report.* "Inflammatory Report," Aug. 3, 1968.

106. Wright, Carlton E. "Summer Participation in the Program of the N. Y. City Council on Consumer Affairs." Unpublished report, Cornell University, 1968.

107. Alexis, Marcus, "Some Negro-White Differences in Consumption," *American Journal of Economics and Sociology* 21 (March 1963): 1-5.

108. Bauer, R. A., and S. M. Cunningham. "The Negro Market," *Journal of Advertising Research* 10 (April 1970).

109. ____ , and L. H. Wortzel. "The Marketing Dilemma of Negroes," *Journal of Marketing* 29 (July 1965): 1-6.

110. Becker, Gary S. "A Theory of the Allocation of Time," *The Economic Journal* (Sept. 1965): 493-517.

111. Bender, Wesley C. "Consumer Purchase Costs—Do Retailers Recognize Them?" *Journal of Retailing* 40 (Spring 1964): 1-8.

112. Berry, Leonard L., and Paul J. Solomon. "Generalizing About Low-Income Food Shoppers: A Word of Caution," *Journal of Retailing* 47 (Summer 1971): 41-51.

113. Brown, F. E. "Price Image vs. Price Reality," *Journal of Marketing Research* 6 (May 1969): 185-91.

114. ____ . "Price Perception and Store Patronage," *Proceedings of the 1968 Fall Conference of the American Marketing Association.* Chicago, 1968.

115. Bruhn, Christine M. "Food Purchasing Pattern of Migrant Agricultural Families," *Journal of Consumer Affairs* 5 (Summer 1971): 41-55.

116. Bucklin, Louis, "Testing Propensities to Shop," *Journal of Marketing* 30 (Jan. 1966): 22-7.

117. Bullock, Henry Allen. "Consumer Motivations in Black and White," *Harvard Business Review* (May-June 1961): 89-104, and (July-August 1961): 110-24.

118. Burgoyne Index. *Twelfth Annual Study of Super Market Shoppers.* Cincinnati: Burgoyne Index, 1965.

119. Crow, Edward L., and Michael G. Van Dress. *Food Retailing in the Cleveland, Ohio, Metropolitan Area—With Emphasis on the Inner City.* Washington, D.C.: United States Department of Agriculture, Government Printing Office, Oct. 1972.

120. Dixon, Donald F., and Daniel J. McLaughlin, Jr. "Shopping Behavior, Expenditure Patterns, and Inner-City Food Prices," *Journal of Marketing Research* 8 (Feb. 1971): 96-9.

121. Dommermuth, William P. "The Shopping Matrix and Marketing Strategy," *Journal of Marketing Research* 3 (May 1965): 128-32.

122. Enis, Ben M., and Keith K. Cox. "Demographic Analysis of Store Patronage Patterns: Uses and Pitfalls," *Proceedings of the 1968 Fall Conference of the American Marketing Association.* Chicago, 1968.

123. Evans, W. Leonard, Jr. "Ghetto Marketing: What Now?" *Proceedings of the 1968 Fall Conference of the American Marketing Association.* Chicago, 1968.

124. Farley, John U. "Brand Loyalty and the Economics of Information," *Journal of Business* 37 (Oct. 1964): 370-81.

125. Feldman, L. P., and A. D. Star. "Racial Factors in Shopping Behavior," *Proceedings of the 1968 June Conference of the American Marketing Association.* Chicago, 1968.

126. Flueck, John A. A Statistical Decision Theory Approach to a Pricing Problem Under Uncertainty. Unpublished Ph.D. dissertation, University of Chicago, 1967.

127. Howard, Ronald. "Dynamic Programming," *Management Science* 12 (Jan. 1966): 317ff.

128. King, Robert L., and Earl R. De Manche. "Comparative Acceptance of Selected Private-Branded Food Products by Low-Income Negro and White Families," in Philip R. McDonald, ed., *Marketing Involvement in Society and the Economy.* Chicago: American Marketing Association, Fall 1969, pp. 63-9.

129. Kohls, R. J., and John Britney. "Consumer Selection of and Loyalty to Food Stores," *Research Bulletin No. 777.* Lafayette, Ind.: Purdue University, March 1964.

130. Larson, C. M. "Racial Brand Usage and Media Exposure Differentials." *Proceedings of the 1968 June Conference of the American Marketing Association.* Chicago, 1968.

131. Martineau, Pierre. "Social Classes and Spending Behavior," *Journal of Marketing* 45 (Oct. 1968): 121-30.

132. Mincer, Jacob. "Market Prices, Opportunity Costs, and Income Effects." *Measurement in Economics: Studies in Mathematical Economics and Econometrics in Memory of Yehuda Grunfeld.* Stanford, Cal.: Stanford University Press, 1963.

133. Morris, William T., *Management Science: A Bayesian Introduction.* Englewood Cliffs, N. J.: Prentice-Hall, 1968.

134. Oladipupo, Raymond O., *How Distinct is the Negro Market?* New York: Ogilvy & Mather, 1970.

135. Oxenfeldt, A. "How Housewives Form Price Impressions," *Journal of Advertising Research* 8 (Sept. 1968): 9-17.

136. Ozga, S. A. "Imperfect Markets Through Lack of Knowledge," *Quarterly Journal of Economics* 74 (1960): 29-52.

137. Petrof, John V. "Attitudes of the Urban Poor Toward Their Neighborhood Supermarkets," *Journal of Retailing* 47 (Spring 1971): 3-17.

138. *Progressive Grocer. Consumer Dynamics in the Super Market.* New York: Progressive Grocer, 1966.

139. ____ . "How Much Do Consumers Know About Retail Prices," 1963, pp. C104-6.

140. Real Estate Research Corporation. *Retailing in Low-Income Areas.* Chicago: Real Estate Research Corporation, 1967.

141. Schlapker, Ben L. "Behavior Patterns of Supermarket Shoppers," *Journal of Marketing* 30 (Oct. 1966): 46-9.

142. Sexton, Donald E., Jr. "Black Buyer Behavior," *Journal of Marketing* 36 (Oct. 1972): 36-9. Reprinted in Ray S. House, Ed., *Readings in Contemporary Marketing.* New York: Holt, Rinehart, and Winston, 1974.

143. ____ . "Differences in Food Shopping Habits by Area of Residence, Race, and Income," *Journal of Retailing* (forthcoming).

144. ____ . "The Utility of Search." Unpublished paper, Columbia University, 1970.

145. Skinner, Richard W. "Consumer Motivation in Supermarket Selection: A Factor Analysis." Unpublished Ph.D. dissertation, Ohio State University, 1966.

146. Social Research *Negroes as Shoppers, Part I.* Chicago: Social Research, 1968.

147. Stigler, George J. "The Economics of Information," *The Journal of Political Economy* 69 (June 1961): 213-25.

148. *Supermarket News.* "Washington Shoppers Shy From Dual Prices." 18, no. 41: 5.

149. Van Tassel, Charles E. "The Negro as a Consumer—What We Know and What We Need to Know." *Proceedings of the 1967 June Conference of the American Marketing Association.* Chicago, 1967.

Grocery Store Operating Costs and Margins

150. *Business Week.* "Writing a Policy for the Ghetto." Sept. 9, 1967, p. 34.

151. ____ . "Writing Insurance for Ghetto Property." Nov. 26, 1968, p. 28.

152. Curtis, S. J. "How to Identify and Control Areas of Shrink." Lecture delivered during Operations Workshop, Super Market Institute Conference on Security, Atlantic City, N. J., May 12, 1969.

153. Donaldson, Loraine, and Raymond S. Strangways. "Can Ghetto Groceries Price Competively and Make a Profit?" *Journal of Business* 46 (Jan. 1973).

154. *Food Dealer.* "Insurance Looms as Major Retailer Problem." Aug. 1967, p. 3.

155. *Food Mart News.* "An Added Expense—Shoplifting." November 11, 1968, p. 5.

156. Garrity, John T., "Red Ink for Ghetto Industries," *Harvard Business Review* (May-June, 1968): 158-61, 171.

157. Ralph Head and Affiliates. *How Supermarket Executives View the Pilferage Problem.* New York: Ralph Head and Affiliates, 1966.

158. Holdren, Bob R. *The Structure of a Retail Market and the Market Behavior of Retail Units.* Englewood Cliffs, N. J.: Prentice-Hall, 1960.

159. National Commission on Food Marketing. *Organization and Competition in Food Retailing, Technical Study No. 7.* Washington, D. C.: Government Printing Office, June 1966.

160. Padberg, Daniel I. *Economics of Food Retailing.* Ithaca, N. Y.: Cornell University, 1968.

161. Partch, Kenneth P. "The Inner City," *Food Topics,* Nov. 1967, pp. 15-30.

162. *Progressive Grocer.* "Shoplifting," June 1961, p. 37.

163. ____ . *Super Value Study.* New York: Progressive Grocer, 1958.

164. ____ . "Your Profit May Be In the Customer's Pocket!" Sept. 1968, pp. 54-65.

165. Sexton, Donald E., Jr., "Food Mix and Profitability: Inner City Supermarkets Revisited." Unpublished paper, Columbia University, 1973.

166. ____ . "Monopoly Profits and Ghetto Food Merchants: An Empirical Test." Unpublished paper, Columbia University, 1973.

167. Simonds, Lois Ann. "A Study of the Variation in Food Costs in Four Cities in Ohio." Unpublished Ph.D. dissertation, Ohio State University, 1967.

168. ____ . "Variations in Food Costs in Major Ohio Cities," *Journal of Consumer Affairs* (Summer 1969): 52-8.

169. Supermarket Institute. "Facts on Security." Unpublished paper, Chicago, May 1966.

170. *Supermarket News.* "Continuing Rioting May End Negro-Area Store Insurance." Aug. 1, 1966, p. 7.

171. ____ . "Detroit Survey Bares Inner City Problems." Sept. 9, 1968, p. 4.

172. ____ . "Employee 'Grazing' Leads to Greener Pastures." Nov. 13, 1969, p. 23.

173. ____ . "Jewel Food Store Future Tied to 'Master Markets.'" March 31, 1969, p. 2.

174. ____ . "Rising Cost of Insurance in the Ghettos—One Approach Toward Solving the Problem." Aug. 1, 1966, p. 9.

175. United States Department of Agriculture. *Farm-Retail Spreads for Food Products, 1947-64.* Washington, D. C. Government Printing Office, May 1965.

176. *Wall St. Journal.* "Heaviest Tax Burdens Said to Fall on Ghetto Homes." Feb. 7, 1968, p. 1.

177. ____ . "A Survey Finds Markups on 'Soul Foods' Are High." Jan. 4, 1968, p. 1.

Competition Among Grocery Stores

178. Alderson, Wroe. "Administered Prices and Retail Grocery Advertising," *Journal of Advertising Research* 3 (March 1963): 1-5.

179. ____ , and Stanley J. Shapiro. "Towards a Theory of Retail Competition," in Reavis Cox, Wroe Alderson, and Stanley J. Shapiro, eds., *Theory in Marketing.* Homewood, Ill.: Richard D. Irwin, Inc., 1964.

180. Baumol, W.J., R. E. Quandt, and H. T. Shapiro. "Oligopoly Theory and Retail Food Pricing," *Journal of Business* 37 (1964): 346-63.

181. Bivens, Gordon E. "An Exploration of Food Price Competition in a Local Market." *Journal of Consumer Affairs* 2 (Summer 1968): 23-32.

182. Black, Guy. "Product Differentiation and Demand for Marketing Services." *Journal of Marketing* 16 (July 1951): 73-9.

183. Cassady, Ralph, Jr. *Competition and Price Making in Food Retailing.* New York: Ronald Press, 1962.

184. ____ . "Price Warfare—A Form of Business Rivalry," in Reavis Cox, Wroe Alderson, and Stanley Shapiro, eds., *Theory in Marketing.* Homewood, Ill.: Irwin, 1964.

185. Church, Colin B. "How Is Newspaper Advertising Used as a Competitive Tool by the Chain Grocers in the Philadelphia Area?" Unpublished M.B.A. thesis, University of Pennsylvania, 1962.

186. Coase, R. H. "Monopoly Pricing with Interrelated Costs and Demands," *Economica,* New Series 13 (1946): 278-94.

187. Fisk, George, Lawrence Nein, and Stanley J. Shapiro. "Price Rivalry Among Philadelphia Food Chains." *Journal of Advertising Research* 4 (June 1964): 12-20.

188. Gorman, William D. and Horishi Mori. "Economic Theory and Explanation of Differences in Price Levels Among Local Retail Markets," *Journal of Farm Economics* 48 (Dec. 1966):1496-1502.

189. Hall Margaret. "Further Reflections on Retail Pricing," *Economica,* New Series 19 (1952): 19-26.

190. Haring, Albert and Wallace O. Yoder. *Trading Stamp Practice and Pricing Policy.* Bloomington, Ind.: Marketing Department, School of Business, Indiana University, 1957.

191. Holton, Richard H. "Price Discrimination at Retail: The Supermarket Case." *The Journal of Industrial Economics* 6 (Nov. 1957): 28ff.

192. Hood, Julia and D. S. Yamey. "Imperfect Competition in the Retail Trades," *Economica* 18 (1951): 119-37.

193. Kitt, Howard. "Entry and Exit in Retail Trade: A Study of Harlem and Bay Ridge." *The Economy of Harlem.* New York: Columbia University, June 1969.

194. Mori, Hiroshi and William D. Gorman. "An Empirical Investigation Into the Relationship Between Market Structure and Performance as Measured by Price," *Journal of Farm Economics* 48 (Aug. 1966): 162-71.

195. Mueller, Willard F. and Leon Garoian. *Changes in the Market Structure of Grocery Retailing.* Madison, Wisc.: University of Wisconsin Press, 1961.

196. Nelson, Paul E., Jr. "Price Competition Among Retail Food Stores—Theory, Practice, and Policy Cues." *Journal of Farm Economics* 48 (Aug. 1966): 172-87.

197. _____, and Lee E. Preston. *Price Merchandising in Food Retailing: A Case Study.* Berkeley, Cal.: Institute of Business and Economic Research, University of California, 1966.

198. Preston, Lee E. "Markups, Leaders and Discrimination in Retail Pricing." *Journal of Farm Economics* 44 (May 1962): 291-306.

199. _____ . *Profits, Competition and Rules of Thumb in Retail Food Pricing.* Berkeley, Cal.: Institute of Business and Economic Research, University of California, 1963.

200. Preston, Lee E. and R. Hertford. "The Anatomy of Retail Price Competition," *California Management Review* 4 (Spring 1962): 13-30.

201. Smith, Henry. "Further Reflections on Retail Pricing," *Economica,* New Series 19 (1952): 26-30.

Examining the Structure of Food Retailing

202. Baumol, W. J. and E. A. Ide. "Variety in Retailing," *Management Science* 3 (1956) 93-101.

203. Berry, Brian J. L. *Commercial Structure and Commercial Blight. Department of Geography Research Paper No. 85.* Chicago: University of Chicago, 1963.

204. Berry, Brian J. L., *Geography of Market Centers and Retail Distribution.* Englewood Cliffs, N. J.: Prentice-Hall, 1967.

205. Clark, William A. and Donald E. Sexton, Jr. *Marketing and Management Science.* Homewood, Ill.: Irwin, 1970.

206. Cox, William E., Jr., "A Commercial Structure Model for Depressed Neighborhoods," *Journal of Marketing* 33 (July 1969): 1-9.

207. Haines, George H., Jr., Leonard S. Simon and Marcus Alexis. "The Dynamics of Commercial Structure in Central City Areas," *Journal of Marketing* 35 (April 1971): 10-18.

208. Hillier, Frederick S. and Gerald V. Lieberman, *Introduction to Operations Research.* San Francisco: Holden-Day, 1968.

209. Kane, Bernard J., Jr., *A Systematic Guide to Supermarket Location Analysis.* New York: Fairchild Publications, 1966.

210. Kelley, Robert F., "Estimating Ultimate Performance Levels of New Retail Outlets," *Journal of Marketing Research* (Feb. 1967): 13-20.

211. Sexton, Donald E., Jr., "Before the Inductive Leap: Eight Steps to System Simulation," *Decision Sciences* 1 (Jan./April 1970): 193-210.

212. ____, "A Graph Theoretic Approach to the Ghetto Market-place," paper presented at 41st National Meeting of the Operations Research Society of America, Atlantic City, N. J., Nov. 1972.

213. ____, "Restructuring the Inner City Marketplace by Simula-tion," paper presented at 40th National Meeting of the Operations Research Society of America, Los Angeles, Oct. 1971.

214. Tapiero, Charles S., "The Theory of Graphs in Behavioral Science," *Decision Sciences* (Jan. 1972): 57-82.

215. ____, Michael F. Capobianco and Arie Y. Lewin, "Structural Inference in Large Organizations," Working paper, Columbia University.

216. White, L. A. and J. B. Ellis, "A System Construct for Evaluating Retail Market Locations," *Journal of Marketing Research* (Feb. 1971): 43-46.

Discussions of Types of Data Employed

217. Boyd, Harper W., Jr. and Ralph L. Westfall. *An Evaluation of Continuous Consumer Panels as a Source of Marketing Informa-tion.* Chicago: American Marketing Association, 1960.

218. Lewis, Harrie F., "A Comparison of Consumer Response to Weekly and Monthly Purchase Panels," *Journal of Marketing* 12 (April 1948): 449-54.

219. Shaffer, James, "The Reporting Period for a Consumer Purchase Panel," *Journal of Marketing* 19 (Jan. 1955): 252-7.

220. Sternlieb, George, "Household Research in the Urban Core," *Journal of Marketing* 32 (Jan. 1968): 29-33.

221. Sudman, Seymour, "Maintaining a Consumer Panel." *Proceedings of the 42nd Annual Meeting of the American Marketing Association.* Chicago, 1959.

222. _____. "On the Accuracy of Recording of Consumer Panels." Unpublished PH.D. dissertation, University of Chicago, 1962.

223. Wadsworth, R. D., "The Experience of a User of a Consumer Panel," *Applied Statistics* 1 (1952): 169ff.

224. Womer, Stanley, "Some Applications of the Continous Consumer Panel," *Journal of Marketing* 9 (Oct. 1944): 132-6.

Bibliographies

225. Boner, Marian O., *The Merchant and the Poor.* Monticello, Illinois: Council of Planning Librarians, 1970.

226. Hafner, W. L., *An Analysis of Research in the Negro Retail Food Market.* Nashville: Joint University Libraries, 1965.

227. Maida, Peter R. and McCay. *The Poor: A Selected Bibliography.* Washington, D. C.: Government Printing Office, 1969.

228. United States Department of Agriculture. *Research Data on Minority Groups—An Annotated Bibliography of Economic Research Reports: 1955-1965.* Washington, D. C.: Government Printing Office, Nov. 1966.

229. United States Department of Commerce. *Bibliography on Marketing to Low-Income Consumers.* Washington, D. C.: Government Printing Office, 1969.

230. _____. *A Guide to Negro Marketing Information.* Washington, D. C.: Government Printing Office, Sept. 1966.

231. United States Department of Health, Education, and Welfare. *A Selective Bibliography of Writings on Poverty in the United States.* Washington, D. C.: Government Printing Office, Oct. 1964.

232. Winters, William R., Jr., Klein, Thomas A., and Brunner, G. Allen, *Minority Enterprise and Marketing: An Annotated Bibliography.* Monticello, Illinois: Council of Planning Librarians, April 1971.

Index

About the Author

Donald E. Sexton, Jr. is associate professor at the Graduate School of Business, Columbia University, where he teaches courses in statistics, marketing, and management science. He received the B.A. from Wesleyan University and the M. B. A. and Ph.D. degrees from the University of Chicago in the fields of mathematics and economics. Professor Sexton has written numerous articles that have appeared in scholarly journals, on subjects ranging from the inner city to advertising, management science, and developing countries. He has coauthored one text, *Marketing and Management Science,* and is presently completing another on marketing research. His current research interests include an investigation of the factors governing the availability of credit to low-income families as well as an exploration of the public policy issues implicit in the findings of this book.